THE
TRUTH
ABOUT
POWER RANGERS
Phil Phillips

THE TRUTH ABOUT POWER RANGERS

Phil Phillips

STARBURST PUBLISHERS

TM

P.O. Box 4123. Lancaster, Pennsylvania 17604

To schedule Author appearances write:
Author Appearances, Starburst Promotions, P.O. Box 4123
Lancaster, Pennsylvania 17604 or call (717) 293-0939

Credits:
Cover art by David Marty Design

The Truth About Power Rangers

First Printing, October 1995

ISBN 0-914984-67-5
Library of Congress Catalog Number 95-69506
Printed in the United States of America

Contents

1

It's a Morphinomenon

Morphinominal!

That's the word that Mighty Morphin Power Rangers use to describe themselves and everything they do.

Others might use the more familiar word, phenomenal. Indeed, Mighty Morphin Power Rangers have accomplished the phenomenal, taking over the afternoon TV, video, action-figure toy, and general product-licensing empire once occupied by the likes of He-Man, She-Ra and Masters of the Universe or the Teenage Mutant Ninja Turtles.

Power Rangers are the new superheroes, the new "big kids" on the tube. And millions of children are watching and emulating their behavior.

What's a Power Ranger?

The *Mighty Morphin Power Rangers* television program is produced by Saban Entertainment.

Haim Saban began his career in Israel, but while working in Japan in the mid 1980s, he spotted a new breed of children's action show on Japanese TV that he thought would work in America. He thought the programs had the campy quality of the old *Batman* TV shows, with bloodless Pow! and Zap! kinds of violence, so he bought the rights to one program, titled *Che Je Yu Rangers*. He took the Japanese fight-scene footage—which featured six brightly-colored and helmeted figures—and added new scenes

7

of young Americans playing high school students, and renamed the show, *Mighty Morphin Power Rangers*. And with this revised product under his arm, he went calling on the networks.

After several years of rejection, Saban pitched the show to Margaret Loesch, president of FOX Children's Network, who bought it and put it on the air in September 1993. Six weeks later, the show hit the #1 spot.

During the past two years, there have even been times when, in a specific region of the nation, 99 percent of all those viewing television at that time period were watching *Mighty Morphin Power Rangers*.

The Power Rangers were part of a massive effort on the part of FOX to gain market share. In less than four years, FOX children's lineup went from nonexistence to holding the #1 slot in both of the children's general categories: ages 2 to 11 and 6 to 17.

Mighty Morphin Power Rangers airs in some markets during the early morning hours, but the main slots are after-school hours. A program also airs as part of the 3-1/2 hour Saturday morning cartoon block. (Loesch would like to see FOX have a Sunday-morning block of time, too.)

Power Rangers is now broadcast in nearly 40 foreign markets. Last season, the program was watched by 70 percent of British child viewers and 75 percent of the child viewers in France.

The program has been classified in a number of ways. It has been labeled a "live-action comedy/adventure sci-fi series." That just about covers the waterfront! In many ways, this is a series that attempts to appeal to everybody.

Peter Dang, president of Saban's Children's Entertainment Group, calls the show a "live-action cartoon" and a "kids' soap opera."

While Power Rangers and their successors, VR Troopers, may be classified as good guys or superheros (the program plays on a young child's interest in dinosaurs, martial arts, and teenage activities), their message is a subtle and dangerous one.

Part 1

Who Are These New Superheroes?

Alpha 5

2

Morphin Time

As with every topic related to your children, as a parent you need to know what you're talking about before you engage in explanation or criticism. If you are going to take on the Power Rangers in your home, you need to know your enemy and why they are an enemy to your children.

In the next few pages, you'll find a "short course" in Power Rangers. We'll take a look at the overall story line, the characters' typical behaviors and routines, and a few sample episodes.

The Basic Story Line

The Power Rangers' origin is a classic mythical battle that supposedly occurred long ago in a far away place.

The wizard, Zordon, led the forces of "good" against the evil Rita Repulsa. The war ended in a tie, however, and Rita and Zordon made a deal to determine the victory with a coin toss. Zordon used magic coins to win the contest, but his victory was not complete. Zordon was trapped in another dimension—locked in a head-view-only column of green light at his Command Center; and Rita (who retained one of the magic coins) and her cohorts were not destroyed, but rather imprisoned on the tiny moon of a faraway planet. After ten thousand years of imprisonment, Rita was freed by space travelers, moved to the earth's moon, and targeted earth as the starting point for her renewed effort to take over the universe.

Hearing of Rita's escape, Zordon called Alpha 5, the robot he placed in charge of operating earth, and ordered him to teleport five of the "wildest, most willful humans in the area" to the Command Center. Alpha teleports five teenagers to the Command Center where Zordon informs them that they have been chosen to battle Rita Repulsa, and are responsible for saving the planet.

Zordon gives each teen one of the magic coins—also called a Power Morpher. He tells the teens that if they are ever in danger, all they need to say is, "It's Morphin Time," then raise their Power Morpher to the sky, call out the name of their designated power source, and they will be "morphed" into a mighty fighter—a Power Ranger! To morph means "to transform into," probably short for metamorphosis, although that is never stated.

Likable Heroes

When not in the guise of Power Rangers, the teens are normal high school students. Each program begins and ends with them in their normal human state.

Jason and Zack are muscle-bound martial arts experts and teachers. Zack also tinkers with cars and gadgets. Trini is into sports. Kimberly is the beautiful popular champion gymnast who is also into gardening. Billy is the kind-hearted super-genius, a true science whiz and computer expert.

All the teens are active in the Angel Grove Youth Center which has a "dojo" or karate training center. All of the teens are skilled in martial arts and gymnastics.

When not engaged in Power Ranger battles against evil, the teens live normal lives. They do what children everywhere dream of doing when they get a older—riding motorcycles, having picnics in the park, scuba diving, and roller-blading.

Not all of the teens in the show are Power Rangers. Two are considered nuisances to the Power Ranger cause—not true enemies, but annoying presences. Their names are Bulk and Skull.

Bulk is the high-school bully, complete with beat-up leather jacket. He is a troublemaker from the start. His pal, Skull, is skinny, dim-witted, and usually wears black-on-black. Bulk and Skull are intent upon discovering the identities of the Power Rangers. They pursue this goal in a bumbling, "nerdy" way. Bulk is a fat teen with more brawn than brains and Skull plays the classic role of the fool.

Other reappearing characters are Ernie, who runs the juice bar at the Angel Grove Youth Center; Mr. Caplan, principal of Angel Grove High School; and Miss Appleby, science teacher. All others are pretty much nameless extras unless they are the featured victims of a particular episode.

Power Access and Limitations

Each Power Ranger teen wears a special wristband to communicate with Zordon's Command Center or with each other. The Power Rangers can also use their wristbands to transport themselves in a streak of light to the Command Center. They also have a jazzed-up VW Bug called the "Rad Bug" that flies them to the Command Center. The Rad Bug can travel from zero to 3,000 miles-per-hour in three seconds and is equipped with a super canon and microwave oven.

The Command Center set is very high-tech. This is the abode of Alpha 5 who has a chipper personality all his own. He routinely greets the Power Rangers as "dudes and dudettes" and when agitated or excited, emits his hallmark phrase, "Ai Yi Yi Yi Yi." From the Command Center, the Power Rangers are able to see events on earth in a glass sphere-viewing globe. This is also where they receive wisdom, advice, and marching orders from the bodiless, green-tinted image of Zordon.

Zordon tells the teens the three rules they must follow as Power Rangers:

1. **Never use your powers for selfish reasons or personal gain.**

2. **Never make a fight worse—unless Rita forces you to do so.**

3. **Always keep your Power Ranger identity secret.**

Catch phrases are at the heart of the Power Rangers "routine." When they sense danger, they declare, "It's Morphin Time!"Then, they hold up their power morpher coins and each teen calls out his or her animal or mythical-creature power source. When the teens have morphed into their superhero identities, they cry, "Let's do it," and vanish, to reappear in the scene of a battle.

Once They Are Morphed . . .

After the teens transform into their Power Ranger identities, they are no longer distinguishable by human characteristics, but rather, by color, weapon, and power source.

Jason becomes the Red Ranger who is endowed with the power of the tyrannosaur. He is chosen by Zordon to be the leader of the Mighty Morphin Power Rangers.

Trini morphs into the Yellow Ranger with the force of the saber-toothed tiger on her side.

Zack takes on the identity of the Black Ranger with the power of the mastodon as his source of strength.

Kimberly is the Pink Ranger with pterodactyl power. (In the new series of shows, her zord is a firebird.)

Billy is the Blue Ranger with the power of the triceratops given to him. (In the new series, his zord is a unicorn.)

As the series developed, a sixth Power Ranger was added to the group. Tommy was initially under the spell of Rita Repulsa. Over a series of five programs, Rita gave Tommy the sixth magic coin to become the Green Ranger. During the series, the Green Ranger sees the error of his ways and chooses to side with good. Zordon and Alpha transform Tommy into the White Ranger who emits a magnificent golden-white aura. Tommy is endowed with the power of the white tiger.

These six Power Rangers are the ones you may have seen on the 1993-94 programs and in most of the rental videos.

At the outset of the 1994-95 season, Jason, Zack and Trini disappear under the ruse that they have been selected to attend a World Peace Conference in Switzerland. Zordon chooses three new Power Rangers to join forces with Tommy, Billy, and Kimberly. The new Power Rangers are:

Adam, a quiet, inner-strength character and master at Kung Fu, becomes the new Black Ranger. His power source is the lion.

Aisha becomes the new Yellow Ranger. She has a repertoire of hip-hop dance moves and is an eternal optimist. Her power source is the griffin.

And Rocky becomes the new Red Ranger. He has a black belt in karate and also teaches martial arts to children. His power source is the red dragon.

With the change in group composition, Tommy, the White Ranger, takes over leadership of the Power Rangers.

Key to Colors and Zords

The color assigned to each Power Ranger correlates to the color of the spandex leotard-style outfit and helmet worn by each when they take on the identity of their "super-selves."

Usually, this transformation is sufficient for the Power Rangers to beat their immediate enemies. When monsters are introduced by Rita Repulsa, however, they need more "zord" power.

The zords look like giant robots made of Legos in the likeness of the animals and mythical creatures cited above. When called by the Power Rangers, the dinosaur powers seem to awaken from prehistoric sleep. Tyrannosaur erupts from a steaming crack in the ground. Mastodon breaks out of a cage of ice. Triceratops charges across a scorching desert. Saber-toothed tiger leaps through a warped jungle and Pterodactyl erupts from the fires of a volcano.

These semi-robotic creatures combine to become Megazord, one super-creature called by Power Rangers to battle Rita Repulsa's monsters which, under Rita's spell, grow to huge proportions.

Megazord has the ultimate power to protect the earth. He runs on a light source; light emanates when the Power Rangers combine their zord crystals to energize the Megazord.

Finally, each Power Ranger has a magic weapon at their disposal that can appear instantly in their hands:
- Trini has Power Daggers.
- Kimberly has a Power Bow.
- Billy has a Power Lance.
- Zack has a Power Ax.
- Jason has a Power Sword.
- Tommy has the Enchanted White Saber.

These weapons can also be combined to make one super weapon—the mighty Power Gun, a crossbow-style weapon capable of firing lightning bolts to destroy the vilest enemy monster.

The Power Rangers also have access to the Sword of Power, which is given to Megazord for the final annihilation of enemies.

(While Tommy is still the Green Ranger, his "weapon" is called the Dragon Flute. Whenplayed, it calls the full power of Dragonzord, a zord that is as big as Megazord but with a powerful tail.)

The Bad Guys (and Gal)

From a fortress established on earth's moon, Rita spies on the Power Rangers with her magic telescope. She uses their human flaws to inflict evil potions on them and cause chaos in their activities.

Rita's character is recognizable by her many "points." She has long sharp fingernails, pointed sleeves and collar, a two-pointed crown, and eerily glowing magic staff. She is routinely called the "Evil Empress," "Your Awfulness," "O Supreme Evilness," or "Your Badness" by the creatures who serve her.

Rita has a variety of robotic goons and wicked creatures to assist her, the fiercest of which is the ruthless Goldar. The Power Rangers consider him to be their fiercest foe in battle.

In addition, Rita has control over the Putty Patrol. The Putties are the creation of Rita's chief monster maker, Finster. Finster creates monsters by squishing clay into evil, living creatures. The Putties appear in grey spandex jumpsuits with grey putty-like faces without features. They do Rita's bidding and routinely engage in minor skirmishes with the Power Rangers on her behalf. The Putties are "disposable soldiers" because Finster mass-produces them, so there's no loss to Rita if they are wiped out.

Actually, any of the Power Rangers, as well as the Putties or monsters, can appear and disappear on cue from Zordon or Rita Repulsa. They can also "teleport" themselves from place to place.

The Basic Action Sequence

The Power Rangers market is primarily four-year-old to seven-year-old children, although the producers claim access to children aged eight to eleven also. Younger children, especially, seem to respond most favorably to the programs' predictability.

The sequence of action in the episodes is also highly predictable. They always open at the local high school, youth center, or dojo. One of the teens has a problem. Rita sends the Putty Patrol to aggravate that problem. There's a Putty fight that could require the teens to morph into their Power Ranger identities. The Power Rangers always defeat the Putties with a combination of karate, gymnastics, and teamwork. Kicks and punches are routinely released with karate "Ki-yaaah" shouts.

After the Putties are defeated, Rita is angered and unleashes a monster to take on the Power Rangers. Zordon usually tells the Power Rangers the monster's ultimate motive and method of destroying the planet.

The result is a monster fight which requires the Power Rangers to have more zord power and possibly weapons. These monsters usually grow to massive proportions. Then, the Megazord is created and a super-monster fight results. That typically ends when the Power Sword is given to Megazord.

That much predictability in plot is tiresome for older children, but young children delight in knowing what will happen next.

The theme song, "Go, go Power Rangers," is repeatedly chanted from the beginning of the fighting until the victory.

Sample Episodes:
Variations on the Battle Between Good and Evil

Following are synopses of four story lines for specific episodes, books, or videos. They are a good overview of Power Ranger tales.

It's Morphin Time

In *It's Morphin Time*, the Power Ranger teens participate in a Cultural Food Fair to raise funds for the Youth Center. The event becomes a food fight after Bulk throws a pie at the principal.

Rita Repulsa is spying on the teens, as usual, and the food fight gives her an idea: create a giant pig monster to eat all the food on earth, beginning in Angel Grove. Rita Repulsa immediately orders Finster to make such a monster.

Although the Power Ranger teens tried to stop the food fight, they are the only teens who stay behind to clean up the mess. While the teens are scrubbing and sweeping, Zordon summons them to the Command Center where he shows them Rita's monster attacking a supermarket in downtown Angel Grove. They engage in battle, but cannot defeat the giant pig monster who consumes their weapons in a few gulps and captures them in a "spin beam." They crash near the Youth Center. Zordon tells Jason by communicator message that the pig is on its way to the food fair, which resumed while the Power Rangers were away fighting the monster. The Youth Center is now in danger of direct attack.

At the Youth Center, the teens discover that Pig-Out created a major mess and moved on to a food-packing plant. The monster left hot and spicy food uneaten. The teens plan to feed the monster food laced with hot peppers. Calling the power of ancient dinosaurs, they again morph into Power Rangers and Trini creates a long hero sandwich laced with peppers and throws it like a spear down the pig's throat. The monster coughs up their power weapons, which they combine to create the Power Gun. They charge the pig, turning him into a shower of sparks and a cloud of smoke.

Rita is more than a little displeased.

As for the food fair, despite two major trashings, the Youth Center takes in almost enough money for new playground equipment. The Power Rangers are able to make up the $20 difference by selling one sandwich for exactly $20 to the principal. The principal fails to see a hot pepper dangling from the sandwich and washes away his toupee while drinking a pitcher of water. Still, he good-naturedly declares the sandwich, "A little hot, but not bad."

Rita's Revenge

In *Rita's Revenge*, Rita Repulsa finds hidden in a cave a chest of magic eggs that can give her universal power. A voice tells her that only an innocent child can open the magic chest. Rita sends her Putties to kidnap Maria, a twelve-year-old girl whom Trini and Kimberly befriended. The Putties whisk Maria to the cave where they and Rita's henchman, Baboo, force her to open the chest. Baboo snatches the eggs and prepares to flee with them to Rita.

The Power Rangers arrive on the scene and face not only the Putties, but a monster named Hatchling—a 70-foot-tall bird-like creature with terrible claws, blood-red eyes, and a razor-sharp beak. The Power Rangers fight the Putties with karate moves, but call Dinozord Power to tackle the Hatchling.

Zordon tells the Power Rangers that the key to demolishing Hatchling is to destroy Romeo, a computer that controls the beast. During the battle between Megazord and Hatchling, the Red Ranger leaps from the Megazord and falls into the open mouth of Hatchling. Inside, the Red Ranger quotes a line from *Romeo and Juliet*, "Romeo, wherefore art thou?" and discovers the location of the computer. He uses the dragon flute to call for help from the Dragonzord, who appears and smashes its tail into Hatchling. That causes Hatchling to spew everything from his mouth, including Jason and Romeo. Jason disconnects Romeo and in seconds, Hatchling's feathers blow away and nothing remains. Restored to teenager images, Trini and Kimberly rescue Maria from the cave.

Meanwhile, back at the Youth Center, Cameron, one of Zack's martial arts students, is competing in a karate match. When Zack is called away on Power Ranger business, Cameron is upset believing he can't win without Zack's support. Zack's responds, "Believe in yourself." Later, as the Power Rangers fight Hatchling, Zack gets similar advice from Zordon, "Be sure of yourselves and use your power." Zack recalls, "That's just what I told Cameron back at the youth center . . . Cameron has to believe in himself and so do we!"

Zack and the other Power Rangers return to the youth center just in time to see Cameron win the martial arts competition.

Megazord to the Rescue!

This story is focused on pollution. Trini leads students to form a club to organize recycling, clean-up, and animal-saving projects. Rita Repulsa responds by creating a monster that will "make their environment so polluted they'll *never* be able to clean it up!" Polluticorn is a man-like creature with a horse face, long mane, gray armor-like skin, giant wings, and a white horn growing from the center of its head.

While the Power Ranger teens clean a park with a combination of gymnastic moves, they are accosted by Putties. The teens defeat the Putty Patrol, but then encounter Polluticorn. They morph into Power Rangers, but Polluticorn deftly fells them. Zordon pulls them to the Command Center just before they are annihilated. Zordon tells them Polluticorn draws its strength from its horn.

The Power Rangers return to earth to keep Polluticorn from trashing their recycling center. They face Goldar and Scorpina, Rita's chief warriors, as well as the monster. With this much evil power against them, the Power Rangers summon the Dragon Shield, a gold barrier formed between the monster and the Power Rangers. Jason manages to swing the blade of his sword against the enemies, cutting off Polluticorn's horn and disarming Rita's allies. Polluticorn begins to grow, soon towering above the tallest building in the city. The Power Rangers must call for Dinozord Power. The dino-robots appear and join to create Megazord, complete with Power Crystals. Still needing more power, the Power Rangers call for the Power Sword, which appears and slices

Megazord's hand. When Megazord strikes Polluticorn with the sword, it disintegrates into a shower of fireworks and flames.

Putty Attack!

The tale begins with the teenagers preparing for a scuba-diving excursion to the beach. Billy and Kimberly stay on shore since Billy is scared of fish. Rita creates a scaly, one-eyed sea monster that emits a deadly poison to the world's oceans to destroy sea life. The monster is aptly-named Goo Fish. Zordon tells Billy and Kimberly about Rita's plan after they encounter six Putties and suspect that Rita must be up to something.

Back at the beach, Billy and Kimberly encounter the Goo Fish and more Putties. Kimberly takes on the monster and Billy the Putties. But then, Rita casts a spell on Billy to increase his fear of fish so he cannot fight. Billy is so terrified, he can't take a step.

The Goo Fish continues its attack on Kimberly while Billy is curled up in fear. Zordon and Alpha 5 make contact with Zack, Jason, and Trini. They morph with dinosaur power and engage in battle against the scaly monster, driving it back to the sea.

The five teens are teleported to the Command Center where Zordon explains what happened to Billy, who is embarrassed that his fear kept him from helping Kimberly. The Power Rangers return to earth and engage Goo Fish in battle. The monster spews goo that slows the Power Rangers and hurls starfish bombs at them. All of the rangers are weakened from the blasts except Billy, who is still immobilized with fear. Finally he recalls, *Zordon told me if I face my fear, I can break Rita's spell.* Billy proudly raises his head and fights with fury. He frees the other rangers and they join their weapons to create the Power Gun and blast the monster.

Rita hurls her magic staff through space to the Goo Fish, which then grows to giant proportion. The Power Rangers call their Dinozords and create the Megazord, that fights with Goo Fish. Jason calls the Mighty Power Sword, which magically appears in Jason's hand. He cuts through the goo cords spewed from the monster, kills the monster, thus returning earth's oceans to safety.

Zordon calls the Power Rangers to congratulate them and Alpha gives Billy a gift: a fishing rod. Billy later comes to the Youth Center with a bag with something squirming inside it. Bulk also appears with a bag, bragging he landed the biggest fish in the lake. Bulk's big fish, however, turns out to be a can of tuna fish. Billy's catch is a lobster that attached a claw to Bulk's nose.

New Foes for the New Season

To keep the show energized for the 1994-95 season, Rita Repulsa has an arch rival, Lord Zed (also spelled Zedd in some materials) who wears glowing metallic red and has a branding iron weapon that leaves a large "Z" imprint. Zed captures Rita Repulsa, tosses her into a dumpster like trash, and hurls it into space.

Lord Zed's sidekick, Squat, is half warthog and half blueberry. Squat is excitable, but not very smart.

Zed has many monsters at his disposal. One, Piranhatishead, has a fish horn that can freeze the zords. He "anoints"—the term used by the Power Ranger creators—Goldar to be his top henchman and restores his wings that Rita Repulsa had taken away.

During the season's episodes, Lord Zed marries Rita Repulsa and a romance develops between Kimberly and Tommy. New special effects are also introduced.

TV is Only the Beginning

Now that you've been introduced to the program and its cast of characters, fasten your seatbelt. The Power Rangers are not only on television. They're everywhere! Even if you manage to turn off exposure to these superheroes in your own home, your children are likely to encounter Power Rangers in many other places.

Here's what you can expect to see . . .

Goldar

3

Chop-Chop and Sing-Along-With-Alpha—
Now Available at the Video Store Nearest You

During the first season the *Mighty Morphin Power Rangers* program was on the air, eight million Power Rangers videos flew out of the video stores!

Power Ranger videos were heavily promoted on the television show and cross-promoted with introductory commercials on the videos themselves. In addition, other videos were offered by Saban Entertainment, including *X-Men*, a series released by Polygram Video based on the Marvel comic series of mutants, and *A Christmas Reunion* from Libra Home Entertainment.

The main Power Rangers video series on the market is a five-part series titled, "Green with Evil." In the video, Tommy, against his will, is sucked into the power grasp of Rita Repulsa. Putties appear from nowhere in a violent assault on Tommy. Even after Tommy defeats them, Rita Repulsa takes control of Tommy using a mystical language and her ability to vaporize people.

Rita Repulsa gives Tommy the missing power coin (the other five coins belong to Zordon's Power Rangers,) and he dedicates himself to the destruction of the Power Rangers. The video does not explain if Tommy knows the Power Rangers in their teen form. Rita wants Tommy to earn the Evil Sword of Darkness so he will be under her control forever.

The series ends with Tommy's conversion to the good side. The other teens quickly "forgive and forget" that Tommy was their arch enemy. He later becomes the White Ranger and the leader of the Power Rangers in the next television season.

Most of the other videos are re-releases of popular episodes.

The videos not only advertise *other* Power Ranger videos, but also the Power Ranger fan club, videos from other producers, and Power Rangers food products—canned pasta, macaroni and cheese, and granola bars—bearing Power Ranger figures on the packaging! The videos also promote *VR Troopers*, the next program in the Saban line. These are classified as "morphinominal," of course.

Two special video releases were issued and promoted by Saban on the episode videos. They warrant your concern.

The Mighty Morphin Power Rangers Karate Club Video

The most problematic of the Power Rangers videos is titled *Mighty Morphin Power Rangers Karate Club* (level 1). It stars the Green Ranger, played by Jason Frank, who is a martial arts expert. It teaches basic karate moves to children as a *program* to develop the mind and become accomplished in the art of self-defense.

The video opens with a lengthy word of caution that it is only for children six-years-old and older, and that the karate moves should only be emulated by children who are in good health, wearing loose clothes, under adult supervision, and on an exercise mat in an open-space area. There is also a disclaimer disassociating the producers from injuries or accidents that may occur.

What is the likelihood that a child *watching a video* will be wearing loose clothes, under adult supervision, on an exercise mat, in an open-space area? Very little likelihood! Most children's television viewing is unsupervised, so children far younger than six years may be watching. And most children watch TV in the living room, family room, or bedroom where lamps, cords, rugs, furniture, and other breakables are often within "kick" range.

By the way, the Green Ranger tells his karate class not to use karate at school in classrooms, hallways or on the playground. But, more than once the Putties are defeated in a school setting.

The video openly says that karate was developed by monks in Tibet and India. It also lists the "Code of the Arts" followed by the monks, all of which sound like "good things" to most adults:

- Brotherhood (and helping others)
- Dedication
- Discipline
- Confidence (believing in one's self)
- Attitude (positive, of course)
- Self-Respect
- Loyalty
- Cooperation (working with others)

What the video does *not* state is loyalty to whom, discipline toward what end, or dedication to what cause. That's an important point to remember as we discuss karate later in this chapter.

The video tells kids to begin with warm-up exercises: modified jumping jacks or "half jacks," "mountain climbers" similar to leg thrusts, running in place, toe touches, leg splits, and high kicks.

Then the "fun" begins. The video teaches some karate moves:

- Square horse stance
- Single punch
- Double punch
- Sweeping block
- Front snap kick
- Back kick
- Tiger stance
- Shuto chop
- Round horse kick
- Front side kick

The goal is to emulate the Green Ranger's "kata"—a series of moves or choreographed sequence of kicks and punches. This kata is the one the Green Ranger usually performs in the fight scenes of *Mighty Morphin Power Rangers*. The entire video builds to the point where a child can *do* the moves of the Green Ranger.

The video is set in a dojo. Periodically, we see cut-away shots to Alpha 5, who expresses enthusiasm with its trademark phrase, "Ay yi yi yi yi." Zordon presents the Code of the Arts information.

What's Wrong with Karate?

Four things are "wrong" about karate for Christian children.

1. Karate assumes each person is completely responsible for his or her own self-defense.

Scriptures teach us the exact opposite—the Lord God is our Bulwark, our Shield, our Defender, our Advocate, our Protector, our Provider, our Rock. Numerous descriptive terms occur repeatedly throughout the Bible calling the godly person to put their trust in the Lord, not in self.

Scriptures also teach that the strong must look out for the weak—to defend and provide for those who are defenseless and without adequate provision. We are not to be self-reliant, but rather, be in *relationship* with others so that we are continually involved in give-and-receive behaviors. Parents have responsibility to defend their children, and adults have responsibility to defend the young. In karate, children may assume they must be solely responsible for their own defense. That's an erroneous position before Christ.

One might argue that a dojo, with its emphasis on cooperation, brotherhood, and loyalty, is like a body of Christians. The appearance is deceiving. Christianity tells individuals to interrelate as members of one body, with each person bearing unique talents and traits. The individual differences are not only accommodated in the body of Christ, but *encouraged*. Karate assumes each person is on the same track, moving through the same set of standards to achieve the "belt" designation of a karate master.

Children involved in a dojo dress alike, act alike and respond to teachers and one another in a highly prescribed set of behaviors.

Karate assumes strength—exerted against outside foes—in *multiplied expertise.* Christianity assumes strength—primarily for the benefit of fellow believers—in *diversified gifts,* all of which operate under the inspiration and direction of the Holy Spirit.

2. Karate assumes that our defense is ultimately "physical."

Although karate makes strong claims that the mind is a person's most powerful weapon, the manifestation of karate is one of achieving definitive victory through *physical* means. One defeats one's opponent through a threat or physical force.

Christianity claims that power resides in the Lord God, and that He "gifts" His people with spiritual power, the highest and purest form. This power does not rely on strength of intellect or physical form. It does not rely on a series of exercises or maneuvers, but is rooted in prayer and obedience to God's Word.

3. Karate assumes that problems which cannot be side-stepped should be dealt with by physical means in a definitive way.

Karate was developed in Hindu and Buddhist monasteries because monks were being threatened and sometimes killed when they traveled. The first course of action in karate is to try to side-step or avoid a problem before it occurs. This step is rarely depicted in Mighty Morphin Power Rangers.

When a problem cannot be side-stepped, physical action is to be taken. If one encounters an enemy on a narrow ledge high in the Himalayas, this may be the only course of action available. But in the routine of playground conflict and school-mate disagreements, side-stepping and confronting are *not* the only options available! At least three other options are usually possible: talking, walking away, or appealing to a person of greater authority.

Power Rangers never attempt to talk rationally to their enemies. They immediately assume their enemies are out for their destruction. Power Rangers never walk away from a fight. They may appeal to Zordon or dinosaur powers for *help* in facing an enemy, but they never assume Zordon will win the battle for them.

Karate forces a child to decide who is friend and who is foe. Karate was birthed by adults, for adults. Adults are more able to discern what behavior is truly menacing and what is just annoying.

Consider a six-year-old child, still egocentric in their world view. That child is learning to share his toys, ideas, and space. Karate assumes that anyone who unlike you—a person not of your dojo—is a potential enemy. Any move such a person might make against your person or property is perceived as a threat. This stance *continually* puts a young child on the defense, appraising others and evaluating behavior. What a burden to place on a young child who should be protected, guarded, and allowed to play and explore the world with a great deal of freedom.

Adults may argue that karate gives a child self-confidence and protects a child against bullies or menacing adults. But karate moves, even if made with all of a child's strength, are not very potent. Most children do not have the muscle mass or coordination to fight with powerful thrusts or blocks. Few children can fight a significantly larger person even with karate expertise, much less several enemies at once. If anything, the "confidence" karate tries to instill in children may be *false* confidence.

It is much more productive to teach a child to communicate with peers, face potential enemies without martial arts training, and discern when to walk away and when to confront. Children also need to be taught when and how to call for help from friends, teachers or other adults, and authority figures (including those wearing uniforms or badges).

Christianity calls for a person to turn the other cheek to enemies and go the second mile in attempting to reconcile with adversaries. Christianity encourages one to resolve differences rather than fuel a feud, reason with foes and win them to Christ, and fight only when the Lord God leads us, along with the entire Church, to engage in conflict that is primarily spiritual.

4. Karate advocates supreme loyalty to the "dojo."

Karate students follow their instructors without question, and with loyalty and respect. In many instances, they are trained to be loyal to their dojo more than any other institution or unit.

Christianity advocates supreme loyalty to the Lord Christ Jesus, and out of that loyalty, loyalty to fellow believers (regardless of their denominational affiliation).

Power Sounds for the Holidays?

Saban Entertainment, specifically Cheryl Saban, produced a Power Rangers video of holiday music titled, *Alpha's Magical Christmas.* It comes complete with a Power Rangers tree ornament.

The premise of the video is that the Power Rangers are away helping Santa, and the robot Alpha 5 is hosting a Christmas party for children from around the world.

The songs, presented with children's voices, include a number of traditional favorites:

Silent Night	Up on the Housetop
Jingle Bells	Good King Wensislaus
Deck the Halls	Jolly Ol' Saint Nicholas
O Christmas Tree	Here We Come A-Caroling
I'll Be Home for Christmas	We Wish You a Merry Christmas

While they sing, children decorate cookies and a tree, join Alpha in making decorations, take a sleigh ride, and distribute gifts. The atmosphere is comfortable, the scenery glitzy.

What is troublesome is the one-world approach in the video. Christian carols are "just some songs" sung at holiday time. The Christmas tree, an image of the Madonna and Child, a sleigh ride, and Santa Claus are put on equal footing. This is a total secularization of Christmas—with the subtle deception of including Christ but not honoring Him as the reason for the season.

Children from around the world, holiday symbols, and interspersed with carols and secular holiday songs, all create a blend that says, "All aspects of the holiday season are equally valid and worthy."

That is demeaning to the Birth of the Savior. Jesus, Alpha 5, Santa Claus, the Power Rangers, and the children are treated as equals. That's blasphemy in the guise of mutual cooperation and international equality.

4

Power Sales

We must never forget that TV programming exists to deliver consumers to advertisers.

Viewers are sold to advertisers. We tend to think that viewers are consumers. In reality, viewers are *sold* to product manufacturers who pay money for the chance to show us their products.

TV programs are not created *primarily* to entertain, educate, or inform. They are created to *attract viewers* by any means necessary. The more viewers who watch a show, the more viewers who watch a commercial. The more viewers who watch a commercial, the higher the fee for airing the commercial and the more money the network and show producers make.

TV shows increasingly have become marketing tools for the sale of product. Think back to the 1950s. *Davy Crockett* aired once a week. Every child wanted a coonskin cap like that worn by his TV hero. The program spawned a product.

Today, a program not only spawns product, but often products are created and a program developed to heighten interest in that product line. The process has been reversed, and on a much larger scale. Merchandising is a primary factor in the creation of children's programming. It is far more important in most circles than the story lines, development of characters, or values depicted.

The average child will see more than 350,000 commercials by the time he is 18 years old. Before a child enters kindergarten, she will have seen 75,000 commercials. Most children watching a half hour of television will see at least seven minutes of commercials.

Do children watch commercials? Studies show they watch commercials at the same attention rate as regular programming.

In programs such as *Mighty Morphin Power Rangers* and *VR Troopers*, many of the commercials are for products directly related to the program. Sometimes, it is hard to tell when the commercial comes on the air. The same music and sound effects, and many of the same visual fighting sequences are used to promote product.

What happens when children see commercials that are intense, high-drama mini-versions of the programs they are watching? They become lobbyists for those products, often demanding the toys, cereals, candy, and other items they saw. The child truly believes these products are part of his rightful domain on this earth. In one study, children under eight years of age were asked to explain why commercials are shown. In another study, children were asked what commercials try to do. (Bever, Smith, Bengen, and Johnson 1975; Robertson and Rossiter 1974; Sheikh, Prasad, and Rao 1975; Warck, Wackman, and Wartella 1977). In both studies, the children couldn't explain the reason for commercials.

Young children don't understand the basic nature of a commercial. They see them as just one more set of exciting visual cues and get the message that they are "supposed" to have what is on the screen. It is not until children reach second or third grade that they understand commercials are designed to sell products. It is not until age twelve that most children understand many of the claims made on the screen about products could be exaggerated.

I was appalled by a quote from Margaret Loesch, the woman responsible for children's programming on the FOX network, in *The Washington Post*. She said as a parent she learned "how important it is for a child to have the toy, or whatever it is of his favorite show or character . . . I only saw one side of it—a toy company trying to make money. I didn't realize the comfort it provided a child."

Now it is not only the desire of toy companies to sell product, TV executives are also telling us that children need these toys for their psychological welfare.

Baloney! A child who *needs* a Power Ranger toy for *comfort* has needs that the Power Ranger toy could never meet.

Artificial Hype for High Sales

Many have rated Power Rangers as the biggest selling toy since Cabbage Patch dolls. The two have something in common: scarcity in the marketplace for a period of time.

Some toys become *more* popular than they otherwise might have because the consumer can't get them. That seems to be the case, in part, with Power Rangers action figures.

Power Ranger dolls debuted at the Toy Fair in 1993. Toys related to upcoming TV shows are sometimes premiered at the Toy Fair held in New York City in February. Buyers can place orders and manufacturers can make product before the shows air the next fall. A popular new show can have a big impact on Christmas buying. Toy buyers try to anticipate which shows and toys *might* become best-sellers long before the shows are seen by children.

That was the case when Power Rangers aired in August 1993. It became *much* more popular than the toy manufacturers anticipated. The boom hit and a shortage of the toys made them all the more popular. The popularity was fueled by the television show, incessant toy commercials, and by *Totally Kids*, a free children's magazine published by FOX. The result was a shopping frenzy. Stores reported throughout 1994 that Power Ranger action figures disappeared as soon as they arrived. One store in West Los Angeles had a waiting list for the toys that extended back several months.

The shortage of Power Ranger toys became so extreme that Bandai America ran national newspaper ads apologizing for the shortage. By February 1994, the company had tripled shipments, but the toys were still selling out. By December 1994, the toys were being manufactured in 15 plants worldwide, 24 hours a day, seven days a week. (They later added yet another plant.)

When Power Rangers toys were hard to find, they were sold from car trunks along roadsides for up to five times their cost. Shoppers reportedly had Rangers "lifted" from their baskets when they were not looking. In other instances, parents took on the task of finding the acessories as a challenge. It is reported that a clerk in a California store had his life "threatened" if he failed to bring home a Power Ranger toy in time for Christmas. He got the toy!

A company spokesman for Toys R Us quoted in *The Washington Post* said, "People are quite aggressive. Parents are sitting down in the aisles, waiting for Power Rangers. They will sit in the parking lots for hours, waiting for trucks to arrive. The minute the truck comes in, they form a circle around the driver, badgering him about what's on the truck. He doesn't know if there are any Power Rangers in there, but they think he does." (June 9, 1994)

Market reports throughout 1994 noted:

- "It was Bandai's Power Rangers, as usual, that dominated demand with the figures and accessories, *when available*, leading the pack. *Dealers hoped supplies would hold up through Christmas.*"[1]
  "Bandai's Power Rangers themselves maintained their bewitched, 12-month sales record. The new nine-inch Whitetigerzord, which combines a white figure and a zord or robot, was an absolute sell-through at $59.99 . . . *but the figure remains hard to get.*"[2]
- "Bandai's Power Rangers remained the number-one item in San Francisco Bay area toy stores *despite continuing short supply* and the appearance of several lower-priced knockoffs."[3]
- "With the Christmas shopping season getting hot and heavy, the most popular lines are pulling ahead of the pack. The Mighty Morphin Power Rangers are the early leaders. Some of the more popular Power Ranger items are videos ($11.99–$15.99), collectible figures ($4.99) and the Power Ranger Action Pal ($14.99). Power Rangers are also emblazoned on activity mats ($9.99),

AM/FM radios ($14.99), toothbrushes ($7.99), and inflatable arm chairs ($5.99)."[4]

When toys become scarce, some parents become obsessed. Parents reportedly telephoned stores for hours a day in search of Power Rangers. Other parents formed "co-ops"—they bought whatever they could find and traded among themselves.[5]

Two Tiers of Product

Some Power Ranger items are directly offered to the consumer by Saban Entertainment:

- Video cassettes of popular episodes, as well as specialty videos of a "karate class" and Christmas party
- A set that includes a cassette, book, trading cards, and 3-D glasses (to pop the karate moves off the page)
- A fan club. Enrollment buys 19 items, including: cards, photos, iron-on decals, a lunch bag, stickers, a video, and membership card. The price is a hefty $17.95 ($18.90 in California and $21.95 in Canada). Some 60,000 children joined the fan club in the first season.

Licenses

Most of the items, however, were manufactured by other companies after they negotiated a license to use the Power Rangers characters and symbols in association with their product.

Since it first introduced *Mighty Morphin Power Rangers*, Saban Entertainment has made more than $1 billion in revenue from licensed products. The Power Rangers are on a faster track than Teenage Mutant Ninja Turtles, which sold nearly $6 billion in merchandise during the first eight years of licensing. Numbers this high are *big* business.

And investment in the licenses paid very well for the manufacturers. Power Ranger items were the hottest moving products and toys in 1994. The hundreds of spin-off products include:

- *Power Ranger Cards*—collectible four-color cards with a Power Ranger scene on one side and a trivia question on the other. To answer the trivia question, a child must have seen a particular Power Ranger show or collected the card with the answer. The first series of cards sold out.

- *Power Ranger Decals*—both metallic and regular decals.
- *Power Ranger Books*—62-page story versions of TV episodes listed at $3.95, published by Parachute Press, a division of Grosset and Dunlap.
- *Power Ranger Caps*—collectible milk caps.
- *Pasta*—Power Ranger pasta was sold in supermarkets.
- *CD Roms*—60,000 were distributed in the first season.
- *Bubble Bath*
- *Bed Sheets*
- *Coloring Books*
- *Jigsaw Puzzles*
- *Pajamas*
- *Paper Plates*
- *Pencils*
- *Stickers*
- *Underwear*
- *Wastebaskets*
- *Doll Set*—for girls, to cash in on the growing trend of girls playing with action-hero dolls. An estimated 30 percent of the Power Rangers figures are purchased by or for female fans. FOX estimates that 45 percent of the viewing audience is female.
- *Video Games*
- *Halloween Costumes*
- *Candy*—specifically Cap Toy's Lazer Pops Sword Candy and the Power Rangers Pin Ball Candy Machine.
- *Hand-Held Electronic Games*

And the list goes on.

In fact, just a few months after the program was introduced, more than 40 licenses had been issued for Power Rangers products. That number topped 85 licenses by the second season.

The 1995 line of accessories is about 50 percent larger than the 1994 line and includes toys based on the movie that is scheduled for release in the summer of 1995.

Some analysts claim that Power Rangers is the hottest license of the 1990s . . . and the decade is only half over.

Toy sales seem to be bearing that out. In November 1994, Mighty Morphin Power Rangers were ranked first in dollar sales of the top-selling licensed properties, ahead of Genesis, Super Nintendo, Barbie, the Lion King, Game Boy and Game Gear, Marvel Super Heroes (X-Men), Batman, and Disney characters.

Of the 20 top-selling toys, Power Rangers had four of the most popular items in December 1994: Auto-Morphin Power Rangers, Power Rangers Karate Action Figures, Power Rangers Sabe the Talking Saber, and Mighty Morphin Power Rangers Deluxe Evil Space Aliens. In November 1994, Power Rangers Red Dragon Thunderzord, Power Rangers Thunderzord Assault Team, and Mighty Morphin Power Rangers 18" Pal also made the top-20 list.

Translated Into Dollars . . .

How do these licenses and standings translate into dollars? First, the accessories aren't cheap. While the action figures broke the $10 industry price trend by selling for as low as $5.99, the vehicles and weapons are much higher priced. The Red Dragon Trapezoid sells from $19.99 to $24.99. The White Tiger Thunderzord ranges from $39.99 to $49.99. The White Ranger set sells at $59.99, and the Saba Sword for $19.95. Both the Power Dame Morphin Playset and the Thunderzord Assault Team sell for $39.99.

Power Ranger videos sell from $7.99 to $14.99, small action figures from $1.99 to $4.99, and board games for $10.99—all of which are priced in the range of affordability for many *children* today. Some of the larger 8-inch action figures sell for $14.99.

From a company standpoint . . .

In a three-month period ending July 1994, Irwin Toy Limited reported net earnings of $1,321,000 (compared to $123,000 for the same period in 1993). The increase was directly related to Mighty Morphin Power Ranger, Mighty Max, and Meccano toys. Sale of Bandai America's Power Ranger items in the U.S. alone reached $300 million in 1994 , a 10-fold increase over 1993 figures.

Power Rangers even impacted Wall Street. When SLM International announced it would sell the toy business of its Buddy L subsidiary to toymaker Empire of Carolina, a company that is licensed to produce some of the Power Rangers figures, Empire shares rose 1/8 immediately.

And most companies holding licenses see yet another mighty wave of sales coming.

Mighty Morphin Power Rangers has high ratings in France and Great Britain, and was seen throughout Europe beginning in 1994. Licensed toys were introduced at the 1994 European toy fairs. Estimates from international toy experts said Power Rangers would become a worldwide brand for at least five years.

The U.S. demand for Bandai's toy products remains at a pace that analysts call "unrelenting." In my experience reviewing toys and children's programming during the past decade, I noted that series such as the Power Rangers seem to have an intense life span of three to five years. After that, the interest begins to wane.

My advice to parents is this: batten the hatches and ride out the storm.

5

Rangers Big at the Box Office

Mighty Morphin Power Rangers are not only found in your television listings, but also on the shelves at your local video store, and in the summer of 1995, at your favorite theater.

As indicated earlier, some of the Power Rangers' popular TV plots were distributed as half-hour videos. Be aware that they are only half-hour videos. Some consumers may think they are buying two hours of video, when each box only has half an hour of tape. The "Green Ranger" series has five tapes. Total playing time for the *story* part of the series, excluding commercials, was only about 120 minutes. The series could have been on one two-hour tape. The series usually costs upward of $30, with each video costing $6.99 to $11.99. Furthermore, the first five minutes of each tape is a non-stop commercial for other Power Ranger products.

Power Rangers on the Big Screen

The 1995 movie is shrouded in silence, but some things seem certain. Lord Zed is more evil. New zords are more exotic and intriguing—computer-generated as opposed to plastic-looking. The new zords include an ape, bear, frog, wolf, and crane, and White Ranger's Ninja Falconzord. The main villain is Ivan Ooze, and like other Power Ranger monsters, he tries to take over the world beginning in Angel Grove. The Putties are replaced with Ivan's minions called the Tengu Tribe.

41

The Power Rangers film was shot in Australia with the Sydney skyline standing in for Angel Grove. The finale includes a Godzilla-style fight. The message of the Twentieth Century Fox film is that of the series—self-esteem. Karate dominates, but the rangers also use devices producers call "non-violent."

Making Their Moves on Stage

The Power Rangers also have taken to the stage for a tour. The sophisticated $3-million live production combines martial arts with driving rock music, and interview sessions when children from the audience can question their favorite Ranger. The show employs state-of-the-art effects and gadgetry, including lasers, pyrotechnics, video towers, giant inflatables, and bombastic speakers. It has a rock concert atmosphere, similar to the "Coming Out of Their Shells" tour that the Teenage Mutant Ninja Turtles did in the early 1990s. The music is definitely rock and roll, in part to appeal to the parents who bring the children.

The tour sold out a 10-day stand at Radio City Music Hall in New York City, and, at present, is expected to visit 80 cities.

The violence in the live show is muted. The combat is so broadly pantomimed, it hardly looks like karate. It's probably because parents, who may not watch the TV show *with* their children, are in the audience. If more parents saw the TV show, more sets would be turned off.

The official name of the live performance is *7-Up Presents Mighty Morphin Power Rangers, Brought to You by Nabisco and Toys R Us.* That says a lot. Before the show, the 7-Up mascot, "Dot," entertains the crowd. After the show, 7-Up contest winners are given free 7-Up and have a meet-and-greet photo session with the Power Rangers. The link between 7-Up and the Power Rangers will continue with the movie and summer 7-Up advertising.

A live show has the potential to sell many licensed items and introduce new ones. The Light Sword ($10) is the most popular item sold at live performances. At some shows, as many as 25 percent attending purchased this item in addition to their tickets, which cost from $10 to $20, depending on seat location and city. Go to a park or zoo instead. You'll save a lot of money and your child will have just as much fun.

6

VR Toopers—Virtually Power Rangers!

VR Troopers could be called the Sons of Power Rangers.

They are the newest generation of TV commandos, also the creation of Saban Entertainment.

The VR Troopers are three teenagers characterized as life-long friends. They are responsible for periodically saving the planet. The Troopers are:

- Ryan Steele, a white male martial arts instructor, whose father disappeared some years ago. (There's no mention of his mother.)
- Kaitlin Hall/Star, a white female photojournalist. (Her name is Kaitlin Hall in the promos for the series, but apparently was changed to Kaitlin Star for the actual programs.)
- J. B. Reese, a black male computer expert.

Tao Chung is their karate instructor at Tao Dojo. Tao is unaware of their VR Trooper identity. Ryan's dog, Jeb, knows their alternate identities. Due to a virtual-reality glitch, Jeb can talk. (Jeb's droll personality is reminiscent of Mr. Ed, the talking horse of years past.)

VR Troopers' wizard is Professor Hart who appears in head-only shots, like Zordon, on a large computer screen in a high-tech lab. He is introduced in promos as a "virtual being" but takes on a much more life-like quality in the series.

Professor Hart admonishes the VR Troopers to work as a team, "stay equal" with each other, and always say "no" to drugs. As in *Mighty Morphin Power Rangers*, the VR Troopers are told to use their martial arts power only for self-defense or to help their friends.

Although the Troopers are told to be equal, Ryan is obviously "more equal" than the others. Each episode begins and ends with Ryan reflecting on times spent with his father.

Ryan also has a more eye-catching outfit after transformation into a VR Trooper. The Troopers wear metallic outfits, with Ryan in red, white, and silver, and the others in silver and black.

Ryan's relationship with his father seems more than a relationship of memory. Ryan is told that his father is "just beyond your reach." Ryan believes his father is still alive, lost or held captive in cyberspace, and Ryan is responsible for his rescue.

What a burden to place upon a child or teen! And think of the message that is sent to young children whose parents divorced. Is it the child's responsibility to find his father and bring him back to reality? Hardly! Not only are the VR Troopers responsible for saving the planet from invasion by virtual beings, they are responsible for rescuing lost and wandering parents also.

Grimlord Leads the Bad Guys

The evil character on the program is Karl Zictor, an extremely rich corporate tycoon who uses a crystal ball and incantation to transform into Grimlord, evil ruler of the virtual-reality world. Zictor's incantation says it all: "Forces of darkness, empower me. Take me back to my virtual reality."

Ziktor Industries is painted as the real-life bad-guy force, just as the dungeon of Grimlord is the virtual-reality focus for evil.

Grimlord's evil "virtual beings" speak to him with the greeting, "Hail, Grimlord." His chief evil warriors are Slice and Dice. That alone tells a potential viewer about the violence of the show.

The enemies in *VR Troopers* are not Putties, but figures called Skugs, who wear black capes with gold trim and helmets. They are a slightly more lithe and mobile version of Darth Vader from the *Star Wars* trilogy.

One never knows what's supposed to be virtual reality and what is reality. The lines are blurry on numerous occasions. But the overall plot seems to be that Grimlord is seeking total control over all the systems of the world by bridging the cyberspace "gap" between virtual reality and reality. It is only with an ability to engage in inter-reality travel that Grimlord can release his virtual-reality monsters onto the earth to take it over.

The program employs computer lingo and many circuitry images. The weaponry includes a "Slashing Sword of Ultimate Destruction" and a "Whirling Blade of Doom."

Many of the combat scenes look like something from a video arcade game with computer-generated air battles. The cyberspace between reality and virtual reality is the primary arena of combat.

To transform from normal teens to VR Troopers, they must hold their magic pendants aloft and say, "Trooper Transform!" followed by "We Are V R!" When the teens return to human likeness, they are said to "retroform."

If all of this sounds highly familiar . . . it is.

Interchangeable Plots and Characters

In many ways, the characters and plots of *VR Troopers* could be interchanged with *Mighty Morphin Power Rangers*. The names, costumes, and places have been altered only slightly.

The Command Center of the Power Rangers becomes the "Sky Base" of the VR Troopers. Both are extremely high-tech in design.

The bodiless Professor Hart of *VR Troopers* is very much like the bodiless Zordon wizard in *Mighty Morphin Power Rangers*. Both are portrayed as omniscient characters, although they are not omnipotent.

Ryan's talking dog, Jeb, is the comic-relief counterpart to the Power Rangers robot, Alpha 5. Rather than say, "Ai yi yi yi yi," Jeb sticks out his tongue (seemingly purposefully and on cue) in derision.

47

Skugs are analogous to Putties in that they appear in pairs and trios, and can take the form of otherwise good people, including traditional authority figures.

The dorky principal in *Mighty Morphin Power Rangers* becomes Woody, the quacky editor of the *Underground Voice Daily* newspaper for which Kaitlin works.

Both programs feature fight scenes that look like they are taped in slag heaps, landfill areas, and on cliffs near the ocean.

Both programs have vehicles that can fly. Power Rangers have a souped-up VW Bug and VR Troopers a red compact car.

Just as in *Mighty Morphin Power Rangers*, *VR Troopers* depicts the good guys in combat with Skugs first, then genuine monsters created by Grimlord. The monsters usually have glowing red eyes.

VR Troopers have their own action-figure toys, of course, with slight variations on weaponry and vehicles. The VR Troopers toys were a hot item for the holiday season of 1994 and are expected to continue to be hot sellers for the next two to three years.

Same Story Second Verse

Not only are the characterizations, settings, and sequence of action similar, but so are the story lines. Here are synopses of five episodes, which are also sold as single videos.

Oh Brother

In the *Oh Brother* episode, two quarreling brothers in the Tao Dojo are taken captive by Grimlord. The VR Troopers are sent to their rescue. When the brothers go through adversity together, they come to appreciate each other and eventually compete in a karate tournament together and win. The message: "Brothers, get along."

Virtual V-6

In the segment titled *Virtual V-6*, the VR Troopers are sent on a mission to protect the environment. Ziktor Industries includes a huge energy empire, and Karl Ziktor is not amused at the invention of a young scientist (once again, nerdy looking and with patched glasses) who has come up with an engine that produces no pollution. In this particular show, the monster is called "Drill-head," an enemy with multiple drill appendages capable of ripping apart both people and things.

Computer Captive

In *Computer Captive*, J.B. is sucked against his will into a computer and ultimately into Grimlord's reality. Grimlord then connects J.B. to a torture device to channel his energy into Grimlord's drones. He is rescued by Ryan just before he dies, and Professor Hart directs a procedure whereby J.B. can be connected to machines in Sky Base that will restore his energy. Teamwork and "using powers to help your friends" is the message of the show.

Lost Memories

In *Lost Memories*, Grimlord has developed a laserbot (combination laser and robot) to try to burn through several layers of reality so that he can unleash his evil warriors into the reality of earth. Ryan fights and defeats Laserbot to save the planet once again. In the process, Ryan loses his memory and must be rescued by his friends. There's no real motivation for what triggers the return of his memory, other than a brief conversation with his talking dog. The message of the show is the importance of hanging onto good memories.

Error in the System

In *Error in the System*, the message is that things aren't always what they appear to be. All of the computers in peaceful Crossworld City are invaded with a virus. It's up to the Troopers to fight that virus . . . which must be done in the cyberspace of the computer world, of course.

The Differences Involve Power

In *VR Troopers*, we find many of the same troublesome messages and symbols as in *Mighty Morphin Power Rangers*. Perhaps the most notable and negative differences are these:

- VR Troopers is much more "explosive" than the Mighty Morphin Power Rangers, literally. Bombs and blasts are common fare, adding to the omnipresent violence of karate kicks and hand-held weaponry.
- Each of the VR Trooper videos ends with a music video that includes visuals far more violent than the program content. The music videos are a non-stop sequence of violent scenes, combat, and explosions, with decapitated figures seen flying through the air.
- The VR Troopers are able to "transfer power" from one to another. They can command force fields. The idea is that the Troopers not only have visible and physical power, but also power that is invisible. This comes very close to a depiction of spiritual power, but with a twist. The VR Trooper power is rooted in the "magic of the pendant."
- VR Troopers has a much higher sexual content. The Troopers themselves are much more physical with one another—arm-in-arm as friends, or an arm of one of the male troopers draped over the shoulder of the female trooper. The show has a number of what I would classify as "better for adults" scenes—for example, teens at a beach in skimpy bikinis. The work-out clothes for Kaitlin are not loose-fitting karate pajamas, but latex gymnastics outfits. (Remember that the biggest fans of these programs are children under the age of 10, with a high percentage of the viewers under the age of 6.)

The other difference, of course, involves the concepts of virtual reality and cyberspace. Whereas Power Rangers engage in a lot of hand-to-hand, or foot-to-face combat, VR Troopers spend a good portion of their fighting time in vehicles flying through cyberspace.

Virtual Reality and Cyberspace

VR Troopers makes the assumption that virtual reality is both a widespread and desirable experience.

Virtual reality is the newest trend in both the electronics and video markets. In the early 1980s, VR was used to help train pilots to visualize objects in graphic three dimensions on a 360° field. The technology was quickly adopted and adapted for use in architecture, design, surgery, and other professions.

To make virtual reality "portable," a viewer must wear special headgear linked to a computer. The projected image inside the headgear fills a viewer's central and peripheral vision with 3-D images that are generated by the computers and respond to the viewer's movement and signals, usually registered by means of hand and finger sensors (often in the format of a gun or other futuristic weapon).

These virtual-reality head-mounted display units are called HMDs. When a viewer's head moves, the view changes. The gadgets range from about $400 to $1,000. Designers are preparing for them to plug equally well into personal computers and television sets.

The first home HMD, called Stuntmaster, was made for Sega and Nintendo systems and released in 1993. It bombed. The new popular unit is called Virtual i-O's i-glasses. Two little monitors display slightly different images which the brain combines into one 3-D view through an optic trick called stereoscopy. The glasses don't try to blanket the entire field of vision, but rather, give the viewer the impression he or she is looking at a large television screen about ten feet away. The glasses are intended to move away from the "helmet" idea to a "glasses" design. The glasses are not only lighter but they are less apt to give a viewer motion sickness. Apparently the weight of HMDs can cause the brain to alter its sense of how to move, creating a sensation those in the industry call "barfogenesis."

All of the major electronics companies (from Paramount Communications, AT&T, Viacom, Sega, Nintendo, Sony, Matsushita, to Edison Brothers, Hasbro, and Time Warner) have placed heavy bets on the success of VR in the next several years. At primary stake are the arcade and home video game markets.

In most cases, what is marketed as "virtual reality" really isn't. True virtual reality allows a viewer to manipulate objects in cyberspace. Most of the games and programs available at present are just more realistic variations of old arcade games or Disney-style rides—techniques that give a new-horizons, touchy-feely sense of reality.

In the case of *VR Troopers*, we need to recognize that "virtual reality" isn't possible using a TV screen. Rather, the plot of the program assumes that the *characters* enter into virtual reality. That translates into TV in some clumsy ways, in my opinion. For example, VR Trooper Ryan rides a motorcycle in "real life." This motorcycle turns into a "turbocycle" in the virtual reality sequences. That isn't an example of virtual reality at all, but rather, simple transformation.

True VR games are interactive, and the more active the viewer becomes, the more the viewer enters into the program. Whereas a film producer is saying, in essence, "Let me show you something," the so-called "spacemaker" or the VR world says, "Let me help you discover something."

Most of the virtual-reality experiences currently available to consumers tend to be short in duration (under ten minutes), and many have a high-tech look, some even showing the computer grid. Viewers tend to report that they feel as if they have been "inside" a video game.

While called virtual *reality*, most of the environments used in the programs are actually fantasy worlds, and so are the figures that occupy their landscapes. The thinking, perhaps, is that fantasy environments can be visually less realistic!

The World of Cyberspace

Cyberspace is the term used to describe the "space" that connects people who communicate computer-to-computer. It is analogous to the term *interpersonal space* we use to refer to the space between two people in face-to-face conversation. Cyberspace has also come to include all of the information available on computer-based networks, such as Internet, America Online, CompuServe, Prodigy, Delphi, eWorld, and GEnie.

Children who are growing up computer literate find "surfing the net"—something their parents or grandparents might call "combing the shelves" or "thumbing through the encyclopedias"—a normal part of computer activity. Parents need to be aware that just as certain books and magazines either need not or should not be read by children, certain information on the "nets" are not suitable for children. Sexual messages, erotica, and pornography—both in text and photo forms—are readily available for downloading onto a home computer (and then printing out). A child only needs to stumble across it or learn how to seek it out.

Teach your child the rules of cyberspace cruising. One of the most important rules is, "Never give out personal or family information, such as a phone number or address." Another is, "Never respond to abusive or suggestive messages." Yet another is, "Always tell a parent if an on-line message is lude, rude, crude, or intrusive." Just as parents teach their children how to use a telephone, they need to teach their children appropriate ways to use a computer. And just as parents should monitor a child's reading, listening, and viewing, a parent should monitor a child's "computing."

There's a helpful booklet available for parents, available free by calling (800) 843-5678. It's called "Child Safety on the Information Highway" and is published by the Interactive Services Association and the National Center for Missing and Exploited Children.

And Coming After the VR Troopers?

In the wake of *VR Troopers*, we're likely to see three more imports from Japan in the near future. Usagi is a 14-year-old girl with special powers, who, with her four friends, regularly saves the world from evil doers. Unlike the Power Rangers and VR Troopers, she is not a high school girl, but a *junior* high student. The responsibility for saving the world is falling on younger and younger shoulders!

Usagi will be renamed "Victoria" for American viewers. Her program is called *Sailor Moon*. It has been Japan's top-rated animated program airing there in prime time.

Two other new Japanese cartoons, *Dragon Ball* and *Tenko*, are also being picked up by American program buyers. *Dragon Ball* features a young boy who has incredible powers and is plunged into mystical adventures in exotic lands. *Tenko* is based upon the performances of Princess Tenko, a popular Japanese magician. Her powers will be greatly expanded for the cartoon version of her act.

It appears that TV station managers are eager to import cartoons such as these primarily because of the ratings success of *Mighty Morphin Power Rangers* and *VR Troopers*. Stations covering about half of the United States have picked up these new cartoon shows for the fall of 1995, even though they were snubbed the previous two years at the National Association of Television Program Executives.

In discussing these programs, Andy Heyward, president of DIC, the animation house that is working on translating the programs for the United States, was quoted in *USA Today* as saying, "The Japanese cartoons have more emotion and more sensitivity in their storytelling. They rely on subtlety, different kinds of artwork and camera work."[1]

More emotion in Japanese cartoons? Yes. But I couldn't disagree more on the other points he makes. The artwork is *different* but hardly what I would call more sensitive. The stories are anything but sensitive. Mary Jo Winchester, a sales rep for Toei

Animation, the company that makes *Sailor Moon* and *Dragon Ball*, admits, "The violence level is different for the Japanese cartoons. We have a lot more weapons and guns."[2]

And *that* fact, openly admitted, should signal concern, regardless of the story line.

Part 2

So, What's Wrong With Them?

7

An Off-the-Charts V Factor

Mighty Morphin Power Rangers and *VR Troopers* are two of the most violent programs ever to be aired to children.

The Violence Factor, or V Factor, is not the only major concern about these programs, but it is perhaps the most obvious to the casual viewer. Children who watch these programs are being fed a *concentrated* dose of violent images underscored with driving, "power" music.

In 1980, National Coalition on Television Violence adopted a standard that ten acts of violence per hour qualified a program as being highly violent. An act of violence is not one fight sequence, but rather, each punch, each kick, each blow, each explosion. I seriously doubt if the average adult could count all of the acts of violence in any one episode of *Mighty Morphin Power Rangers* or *VR Troopers* without the benefit of instant replay. These programs are literally off the scale when it comes to violent behavior.

I'm not alone in criticizing the Power Rangers. Here's what three others have had to say:

Peggy Charren, founder of Action for Children Television:

"It's not so much the violence that kids like about *Power Rangers*, it's that the show starts out with real teenagers that they can relate to. It also draws in girls who think Jason (the ex-Red Ranger) is cute. But when the Ninja Turtles were popular, kids were hitting each other over the head with toy Ninja Turtle swords. Now we're going to see more of these types of playground incidents."[1]

LeVar Burton, host and executive producer of *Reading Rainbow* on PBS:

"I've got a problem with *Power Rangers*. It's a show for kids that offers violence as the only means of conflict resolution. It's bad role modeling and it's irresponsible programming."[2]

Adam West, star of the 1960s *Batman* series and author of *Back to the Batcave*:

"What I see on *Power Rangers* is a story that sets up the violence. The MTV-style cuts and the sound all heighten the impact and make it seem exciting. *Batman* was a comedy adventure — the focus of each show was on solving the mystery and finding the bigger-than-life villains. The fighting was incidental, not presented in a gratuitous manner as it is on *Power Rangers*. The only problem I remember with watchdog groups and *Batman* was when some kid put on a cape and jumped off a building."[3]

Furthermore, the producers of these programs readily admit the violence level is high . . . they simply dismiss completely the impact that the violence may have.

FOX executive Margaret Loesch finds *encouragement* in the fact that while the Power Rangers have been criticized by members of the press for the violence in the shows, neither parents nor teachers have criticized the programs, either in large numbers, individually or through organized parent and teacher groups.

Loesch says her own standard rule about violence is that it should not be of the sort that could be imitated by a child to his harm. She cites an instance with her own five-year-old son. When she found him imitating the karate on *Mighty Morphin Power Rangers*, she says:

"The minute he jumped up and started pretending he was a karate expert, I said, 'You can pretend to be playing karate, but you don't go out and chop the cat and you can't hit your friends. That's unacceptable. This is a fantasy and it's only television. And he understood."[4]

Yeah, sure.

In the January 1995 issue of *Playthings*, Trish Steward, director of marketing at Bandai America made this statement about the controversy surrounding the violence depicted on the Power Rangers programs:

> "Over the last 10 years, the industry has seen issues of violence, usually tied in to whatever is successful. Then it calms down. Saban (the show's creator) has done a good job with public service announcements."[5]

Statements such as these send chills down my spine. What is happening is that the producers of these programs and the manufacturers of the toys related to them see no problem with violence being used to "entertain" children or to excite them toward the purchase of a product.

Have we really become so insensitive as a culture to the debasing impact of violent images? Have we really become so desensitized to the very issue of violence?

I fear that we have.

When I speak about children's toys and programs, I am finding more and more that parents seem to "turn off" when the word violence is mentioned. The statement "too much violence" is sounding like a broken record, and sadly, people no longer pay attention to warnings about violence.

That does not make violence any less of an issue or any less detrimental to children.

What Do We Know About Violence?

Let's briefly review what we know through many scientific research studies about the impact of violence on our children.

We need to recognize at the outset, of course, the way science functions. It's very difficult to prove cause-and-effect relationships. Most research studies come up with "correlations" —which means the likelihood or probability that one set of behaviors is linked to another.

Even so, what we know from the research is plenty alarming. Let me summarize just a few of the findings for you.

1. **A study is yet to be conducted that proves there is no relationship between television violence and real-life acts of aggression.**

Even the most liberal of studies concludes that while aggressive behavior is "unlikely," television "could precipitate it in those few children who are emotionally disturbed." Alberta Siegel wrote, "Viewing the carnage does not guarantee that the viewer will go forth and do likewise, but it raises the probability that he will."[6]

2. **More than 50 studies concluded that the more violence a child watches, the more aggression a child displays.**

Since 1982, TV violence has increased 780 percent. During that same period, teachers report a near 800-percent increase in aggressive acts on playgrounds. Scientists are reluctant to say that the two sets of behaviors are related, but common sense concludes, "There's obviously a connection."

3. **Children who watch violence tend not to display aggression if there's a mitigating circumstance.**

In other words, if a parent says "no" to aggression—or a teacher or other adult in authority—then the child is far less likely to display aggression. However, if a child watches violence by himself and there's no one around to say "no" to such behavior, the child is more likely to display aggression. What does this tell us about latch-key kids, or children raised in tenements who watch 12 to 14 hours of television a day without any parental supervision, parental input, or other parental "mitigation?"

4. **A child is more likely to be aggressive if the violence the child views is the kind that causes serious injury.**
(Berkowitz and Alioto 1973; Green and Stonner 1972).

One of the most common definitions of violence is that of Gerbner, a major researcher in the area of TV violence and child aggression. Violence is "the overt expression of physical force against others or self, or the compelling of action against one's will on pain of being hurt or killed." It's not violence if a person accidentally falls down the stairs. It is violence if a person is "pushed" down the stairs!

What happens to enemies on *Mighty Morphin Power Rangers* and *VR Troopers*? They are annihilated. In many instances, the end result is a cleverly disguised form of death—the battered and defeated foes appear to be electrocuted and then disappear. Since the Putties on the Power Rangers program are manufactured in assembly-line fashion, their disappearance isn't considered real "death" to the adult producers. The Putties vanish and others are created to take their place. One can't help but wonder how a child perceives this.

The monsters on *Mighty Morphin Power Rangers* do die, usually in a massive explosion or combat action.

The programs are laden with pain and physical defeat, all of which are intended not only to cause injury, but to result in *destruction*. Power Rangers and VR Troopers don't tie up their enemies, imprison them, or bring them to a court of justice. They annihilate them.

5. Aggressive behavior is more likely to occur in children when the violence they watch is seen as part of a highly exciting environment.
(Tannenbaum and Zillmann 1975; Zillmann 1971).

What makes for excitement? Usually close-up shots, unusual camera angels, sophisticated film editing techniques, a steady undercurrent of music, and realistic sound effects. These are the tools of the producer to amplify excitement. Violent acts are often portrayed using these techniques so that the violent action becomes something of a climax, with the end resolution being one of no music, normal behavior, no sound effects, and a return to "calm."

This is the pattern of every Power Rangers and VR Troopers program. As the violent actions escalate, so does the music, the rapid cutting from scene to scene, and the number of sound effects.

One of the things that continues to amaze me year after year is that although violence is denounced, it is never eliminated! As far back as 1968, the National Commission on the Causes and Prevention of Violence stated, "We believe it is reasonable to conclude that a constant diet of violent behavior on television has an adverse effect on human character and attitudes."

Yet TV programs became more violent.

In December 1975, the *Journal of the American Medical Association* featured an article by Dr. Michael Rothenberg, a noted Seattle pediatrician, who wrote about TV violence and called for "a major organized cry of protest from the medical profession in relation to what, in political terms, I consider a national scandal" (p. 1043).

Yet nothing happened.

The national PTA organization launched a campaign against TV violence in 1976, joining forces with the American Medical Association. The amount of violence on TV dropped in 1977, but the decrease didn't hold.

The Escalating Cumulative Effect

Through TV, we Americans teach violence to our children to an extent that no young people in any other nation, or at any other time in history, have been taught. In fact, children's programming is five times more violent than prime-time shows, which have a high violence rating as a whole.

The latest statistics compiled by the American Psychological Association tells us that the average child watches up to 8,000 made-for-TV murders and 100,000 acts of violence by the end of grade school![7]

The FOX network leads NBC, ABC, and CBS in the "average violent incident per hour" rating for all programming with 5.92 incidents. This average, of course, includes talk shows, soap operas, and news shows, meaning that the bulk of violence is actually appearing in prime-time and on Saturday mornings, times when children are a large part of the viewing audience.

The average number of violent acts per hour on Saturday-morning children's television now stands at 22.8. The percent of Saturday-morning programs containing violence is 94.7 percent. In other words, it's nearly impossible to find a Saturday-morning program that does NOT have violence in it![8]

Twenty-five percent of each episode of *Mighty Morphin Power Rangers* is considered to be "violent." That means one quarter of each half-hour program actively portrays violent actions. That's an amazing percentage! And, it doesn't count the commercials for Power Ranger products. Some of those are even more violent than the episodes themselves.

Two False Assumptions

These figures are startling, yet even in the face of them, parents tend to make two false assumptions:

False Assumption #1: One program is OK.

That isn't necessarily so. Why feed your child *any* violence? That's like saying feeding a child just one capsule of high-blood-pressure medicine from Grandma's pill box is OK.

What a parent needs to recognize is that few children see or encounter "just one program." Most children are fed an entire smorgasbord of these shows. The *cumulative effect* is what is staggering.

The problem, however, is that shows are put on the air one at a time. To come against any one program is perceived as railing against that show. Ten other shows only slight less violent are waiting in the wings to take its place if it is removed from the schedule.

When parents allow their children to watch "just one show" they are sending a message to TV producers that *their* program may be the show you will allow.

False Assumption #2: My child won't act in a violent way if he doesn't have access to weapons.

I have met a number of parents who assume that their children will *not* show aggressive behavior in real life because they have no guns in the house. Some claim that since they don't give their children toy weapons to play with, they won't become violent as adults.

Don't count on that.

In the first place, the new trend is not toward guns—but toward explosives. In fact, it may be far easier for a child to make a bomb than to gain access to a gun.

In January 1995, the *Dallas Morning News* reported that a 13-year-old boy was seriously injured when he ignited a home-made pipe bomb. Where did he learn to make such a bomb? From an electronic bulletin board accessed by a home computer! Text-based copies of books telling how to build bombs are commonly available on local computer bulletin boards or on Internet (the unregulated international network). Many of the articles and books, such as the controversial *Terrorist Cookbook*, often label the information they give as theoretical, yet they include step-by-step instructions.

What Will It Take?

What will it take to end violence on television?

The solution is simple, but apparently oh-so-difficult to do.

Parents need simply to turn off the television sets in their homes when violence is broadcast. And parents need to do this en masse.

That, and ultimately that alone, will send the signal—TV violence will *not* be viewed by our children. When that happens programming will change because producers want to air pro-grams that are watched in order to sell commercial time so that products will be sold.

As long as parents allow their children to watch TV vioence . . . as long as they allow television sets to remain on when violent programming is aired . . . nothing will change—except that the programs are likely to become more violent.

Fear and Desensitization

Violence on television causes more than aggressive behavior in children. It also creates fear. Studies have found that children who watch violent television programs are more scared about their worlds at large, more frightened that someone bad will come into their homes, and more afraid they will be hurt when they leave their homes, than children who do not watch violence. (Biblow, 1973)

Young children, especially, are not able to distinguish between reality and fantasy. To the young child, what happens on the screen *is* real, in spite of what a parent or older child may say about it. Dr. Glenn Sparks of Purdue University, was quoted in an interview as saying,

> "Between the ages of seven and eleven, children frequently mention that violent TV scenes frighten and upset them. Children this age realize these scenes could really happen—and happen to them. They're not ready to cope with this yet."

Fear actually makes a child feel that he or she has less control over a situation. It's ironic that a show aimed at showing power to children might actually make children feel that they have less power or inability to escape a dangerous situation.

Violence can also result in desensitization. This is not just a psychological idea, but a fact rooted in physiology. When a child sees violence, very real things happen in the child's body. One might expect the heart rate of a child to increase during violent acts. In fact, studies have shown that the heart rate of younger subjects decreased, with young children showing a greater decrease than older children (Surbeck 1973). This is a defensive mechanism! The children are responding physiologically in a "flee" mode, even though everything about the scene, music, and sound effects encourages them to "fight."

67

When a child experiences this kind of conflict—physiologically shutting down but psychologically "coming alive"—tension results. The child feels anxiety, an uneasiness, stress. Young children don't know how to deal with stress. Their normal response is to act in ways that an adult might call "bouncing off the walls." They turn first to one thing and then to another to try to resolve the inner tension they are experiencing. Eventually, the child tends to resort to a general pattern: behave actively, but don't "feel" anything as you do. This is a highly dangerous state for any person! When a person chooses to behave in an outwardly vigorous way, yet without emotion, raw aggression is likely to be the result.

Erma Bombeck once wrote an angry open letter to the television networks in which she said:

> "During a single evening I saw twelve people shot, two tortured, one dumped into a swimming pool, two cars explode, a rape, and a man who crawled two blocks with a knife in his stomach. Do you know something? I didn't feel anger or shock or horror or excitement or repugnance. The truth is I didn't feel. Through repeated assaults of one violent act after another, you have taken from me something I valued—something that contributed to my compassion and caring—the instinct to feel."[9]

When we feed our children violence, we destroy that instinct at an early age. Is it any wonder that we have so many teenagers today who commit highly violent acts and then say they, "didn't feel anything" while committing them?

The Bigger Picture

Consider some of the facts related to our society as a whole. The present generation is:

- killing itself at a rate that reflects a 300 percent increase over the previous generation. The murder rate of black youths aged 14 to 24 in the USA is four times greater than that of any other industrialized nation on earth. Black youth, sadly, are many times more likely than white youth to watch large doses of television without mitigating circumstances (that is, parental involvement). The growing trend extends to poor white youth, also often left home alone with a violent tutor called TV;

- experiencing rape of women at a rate that reflects a 500 percent increase over the previous generation;
- assaulting one another at a rate that is 600 percent more often, per capita, than the previous generation.

Child abuse is growing in proportion to the general population. The number of people imprisoned is growing in proportion to the general population.

How can any argument be made for showing *any* violence to our children, or for that matter, to ourselves?

If we truly want to live in a more peaceful world, a good step in that direction seems to be to depict a more peaceful world to our children.

A Test for Violence

For years, I have recommended this **five-fold test** for evaluating the violent content of a child's program:

1. Count the number of weapons in the cartoon and try to keep track of the number of times each is used. If more than three weapons are used or one weapon is used more than three times, turn it off. In the case of any program using martial arts, consider the karate moves themselves to be weapons. Legally, they are. The hands and feet of a black-belt karate expert are classified as lethal weapons.

2. Count the number of people killed. If anyone is killed—or eliminated, annihilated, destroyed—turn off the program.

3. Count the number of unprovoked attacks (whether the character is good or bad). If there are any, turn it off.

4. How do the good characters resolve conflict? Do they use the same methods as the bad guys? If so, turn off the show.

5. Do the good guys break laws, even with so-called good motives? If so, turn off the TV.

We can't expect the government to regulate what our children watch. It sounds like a good idea, but it simply won't happen.

Programs such as *Where in the World is Carmen Sandiego?* and *Ghostwriter*—both of which have won high praise from children's advocates—cost as much as $390,000 per 30-minute episode, which is far more than many non-educational programs. Many of the animated action shows have advertiser tie-ins to offset costs. The more educationally-oriented programs tend not to have tie-ins, and thus, less revenue associated with them.

The Federal Communication Commission proposed that more air time be given to instructional fare as part of the Children's Television Act of 1990. Government officials were immediately hounded by television executives and producers. The FCC favored a ruling that barred programs, such as *The Jetsons*, from being classified as "educational." TV executives claim that if a program teaches values that are good, in spite of other aspects of the program, the program should be considered instructional. Indeed, that's the way the ruling is expressed. Any show that advances "the positive development of the child in any respect" qualifies it as educational programming. By such a definition, of course, virtually all programming could be construed to have at least *some* instructional merit, even if the program is teaching children what *not* to do!

In the end, money talks and good taste walks . . . out the door.

And in the end, it's the parent's responsibility to control the use of the television set just as the parent might control the use of the family's chain saw or lawn mower.

8

What the World Doesn't Need Now is Another Gang

Power Rangers and VR Troopers are two more examples of "gang" behavior on television.

Every child wants and needs a circle of friends, but what our society doesn't need is more gangs.

What distinguishes a gang from a normal group of friends?

1. Loyalty to the gang overrides any other loyalty.

Specifically, loyalty to the family or society as a whole. Power Rangers are depicted as having other acquaintances, but no other genuine friends. They are a closed group, loyal primarily to one another. The same for the VR Troopers.

2. Gang members are all within a narrow age range.

Power Rangers and VR Troopers appear to be members of the same class in their respective high schools.

3. Third, gangs generally have an older and wiser person who is the "wizard" for the group.

This "wizard" may be older and street-smart, but never a family member. Zordon certainly qualifies as this for the Power Rangers. Professor Hart and Tao Chung qualify as virtual reality and true-life wizards for the VR Troopers. These "older and wiser" figures do not live or actively engage in the world of those they advise, which is typical of gang gurus. They supervise from a

71

distance. They never fight, but rather, send or train others to do the dirty and dangerous work.

4. The gang is usually identified by a common uniform, emblem, slogan, or secret code words.

Power Rangers have Power Morphin coins, slogans, and brightly-colored neon spandex outfits. VR Troopers have hard-metal outfits, VR pendants, and slogans. Power Rangers wear common wrist "communicators."

5. A gang has "turf."

This turf must be defended at all costs, even the cost of life. For Power Rangers and VR Troopers the turf is the entire planet. Still, defense of the turf repeatedly requires these teens to risk their lives.

It's also important to note that gangs take root and survive because they provide a sense of affiliation that a child doesn't otherwise experience. The gang becomes the child's "family." Unfortunately, it's a family of all siblings with no moms and dads.

Where is the Family?

The nuclear family doesn't exist in either of the *Mighty Morphin Power Rangers* or *VR Troopers* programs. That's true for most children's programing. When non-wizard adults are shown, their characters are often trivialized, such as the case of the off-beat principal on the Power Rangers. In other instances, the missing parents are immortalized. This happens with VR Trooper Ryan Steele. His father is missing for a number of years and Ryan ardently desires to find his dad, who appears to be in another time or space dimension related to virtual reality. Each episode of *VR Troopers* opens with a scene of Ryan's childhood with his father, and closes with a sentiment related to his missing father.

In cases of impending tragedy, parents are never consulted on programs such as *Mighty Morphin Power Rangers* or *VR Troopers*. The teens must defend themselves, their schools, families, neighborhoods, and nation. And in the case of these two programs, the planet. The child-as-savior is a troublesome concept. Yet this theme is reinforced by many cartoons and movies.

Two of a child's prime fears are that his peers won't like him and that he will be left alone. The importance that TV places on gang affiliation does little to alleviate either fear. Indeed, the research evidence leads one to believe it promotes these very fears. A child's basic "security group" is not intended to be a gang, according to God's Plan, but rather, the family. The child who grows up with strong family ties has far less fear of rejection or of being alone. As adults, we need to give our children a supportive family environment. But we also need to present models of other strong families to our children, thus eliminating the need for a "gang" to provide identity, safety, love, or understanding.

It's ironic that TV places such importance on peer associations when TV itself is primarily a "loner" activity that separates children from other children.

A Parent's Challenge

Parents need to provide a loving family atmosphere for their children, also a circle of friends. Join with other families to create friendship groups for your child. Take turns hosting children in your home so they can play and work on projects together.

Get your child involved in Sunday school and youth group activities at your church, perhaps including a Scouting-style program or children's choir.

Get your child involved in community activities as a volunteer. Even young children can hand out sandwiches to the hungry.

Get your child involved in a sports program of their choosing. That sport may be chess or a rugged team sport. Choose activities that involve cooperate effort and team work.

Get your child involved in taking lessons to enhance their natural abilities. Group lessons are less expensive and give a chance for them to be friends with kids who have similar interests.

The child who is actively engaged in play, work, study, and growth with "friends" is not a child who needs a "gang."

Superheros

Power Rangers

9

Copycat Play

Children copy what they see on television. They copy mannerisms, behavior, and the way the characters interrelate. When a child is given a toy related to a television show, they will naturally engage in "copycat" play. They are likely to play with the toy the way the figure acts on television.

Children often re-enact pretold, prepackaged stories when playing with action figures related to television shows. They are simply retelling the story, over and over. The characterizations are in place. The mannerisms and plots were demonstrated to them and engraved in their memories. This isn't play. It's performing.

Remember that toys related to *Mighty Morphin Power Rangers*, *VR Troopers*, and other programs of this type, are tiny figurine and weapon replicas of what is seen on television. When children play with these plastic figures they play with the television characters they represent, including the monsters. This form of play does several things to a child.

1. This type of play greatly stifles creativity.

Good toys cause a child to make up stories, develop characters, try on "pretend" roles, and compare them to reality. A good toy will develop a child's ability to communicate and reason, and improve eye-hand coordination.

A doll with no name can become *any* person of any age, culture, or period in history. A Power Ranger or VR Trooper comes with an identity set in a narrow frame of reference.

2. This type of play limits a child's ability to make choices.

One great lesson learned through "play" is how to make choices. If the playscript was written for a child, those choices are highly limited. A child playing with a VR Trooper doll is unlikely to explore the options available to a person facing an enemy. The method of response is prescribed and the reaction is "programmed."

3. This type of play limits a child's development of humor.

Through unstructured and creative play, a child develops a distinctive sense of humor. There's little humor in *Mighty Morphin Power Rangers* and *VR Troopers* except occasional slapstick, pie-in-the-face, physical moments in their world. The characters are a serious bunch. After all, saving the world takes effort!

Most examples of humor are not ones I want my children to copy. Both programs have sarcastic insults such as Grimlord refering to his own "bots" (robots) as "incompetent pieces of scrap metal." Not much to build self-esteem in that remark.

In *Putty Attack*, Skull hooks Bulk's pants with his fishing line and reveals Bulk's rainbow-colored underwear. Again, not what I want my children doing on the playground.

It's interesting to me that while adults speak of a child's years as being "carefree" and "years for fun," most of the stories in children's programs today are not funny or fun-filled. They are dramas,written in dramatic mode, and rooted in conflict. They do not show human foibles or the innocent pranks and pitfalls of normal childhood. Rather, they emphasize would-be hoped-for omnipotence over issues far larger than those encountered by the vast majority of kids.

4. This type of play distorts a child's concept of time.

Children who are fed heavy doses of television,reinforced by play with television-based action figures, tent o expect problems to be solved and projects accomplished within minutes. The Power Rangers can defeat even the most awesome monster in undrer five minutes. In play, children adopt this same time frame, often hopping from one monster to another within minutes. Is any thoujght given to carefully mapping out strategy or to engageing in a plot that takes longer than a few minutes to resolve? Raely.

Alternatives for Parents

What can a parent do? First, parents should choose slower-paced programs for children. "Mister Rogers," the classic PBS production, is a good program for young children, as are Winnie the Pooh stories. These programs emphasize cooperation, compassion, and kindness. Christian videos also are available.

Emphasize books over TV. Literacy is more than knowing the alphabet. It is understanding how words are put together. Expose your child to magazines, maps and books. Make library visits a regular activity.

Watch TV with your children. Point out meaning, give context, and help them understand a character's motivation. Use TV as a tool to trigger "add on" stories and help your child conjecture what may have happened next or as a result of the story. Get your child thinking about a new plot. Look up places that are mentioned in a program. Build upon concepts that are related to a child's learning of the alphabet and numbers.

Choose activities other than TV to promote learning skills. Take walks and encourage children to play and make up games. Encourage self-motivated play with toys of their own creation. Buy toys that "have no name." Let your child give his or her dolls names and identities. Let a box become a fort, a packet of sidewalk chalk the means of defining a house. Choose toys that require your child to make up plots and take on roles.

Don't let a television do all of your child's thinking or imagining for him. If you do, your child's thinking will go down the drain . . . and your child's imagination will be greatly stunted.

Putty Patrol

10

The Catechism from the East

The best enemy of excellence is "good." Don't settle for want-to-be values. Go for the real thing!

Power Rangers' material expresses a number of values—either given orally by the heroes or by implication of outcome—that most Christian parents would embrace:

- Power Rangers give everything their best shot, regardless of situation (according to a statement on a card pack).
- Power Rangers advocate togetherness, teamwork, loyalty, and cooperation.
- Power Rangers fight evil.
- Power Rangers are politically correct, almost precisely so. The original Rangers included one Asian, one African-American, and one Latino. Of the six Rangers, two are girls. One of the boys has a ponytail. The new Rangers have pretty much the same mix of races.
- Power Rangers are strong advocates of mutual respect and they display good manners (at least toward one another).

These factors might be considered important to a parent, regardless of how Power Rangers spend the bulk of their time—which is kicking, elbowing, punching, and otherwise karate-chopping or blasting their enemies into oblivion.

The underlying motivation of the program, however, is where the problem lies.

From Which Root System?

Mighty Morphin Power Rangers is the shared vision of Cheryl Saban and husband, Haim, (chairman and chief executive officer of Saban Entertainment). Cheryl, mother of two young children, is the principal writer of the show. She was quoted as saying:

> *"Power Rangers* is full of action and physicality. It is not preachy, but it does have a subtle moral fiber that children can embrace."[1]

The fact is, however, not all "moral fibers" are created equal. Similar ethics or ways of behaving can come from very different sets of beliefs and values.

Consider a typical orchard. The trees may have things in common: they may all have leaves, bark, branches, and twigs. They may even all bear apples. Yet, some of those apples may be Granny Smith and others Winesap and others Golden Delicious. The saplings came from different seeds or root stock.

Not all "ethics" come from the same root system. The root system for Power Rangers' values is from the Orient and steeped in Far-Eastern values and beliefs.

How Much Cultural Diversity Is Good for a Young Child?

The "brotherhood and cooperation" theme of Power Rangers is grounded in the concept of cultural diversity and mutual acceptance of all cultures as being equal.

FOX executive Margaret Loesch has openly stated this, believing that the trend toward more Japanese cartoons is a good one:

> "It reiterates that good product is made all over the world. We Americans tend to think that things are only good if they're made here. But it's a big world, and we owe it to our kids to show them more cultural diversity."[2]

I certainly am not opposed to cultural diversity. We are living in a shrinking world, one in which communication technology is more readily available than ever before, and the *need* to communicate has never been greater.

One thing we must openly recognize is that culture can be defined in various ways. It can be narrowly presented to focus on differences in: customs, food, clothing, architectural styles, language, methods of schooling, transportation, and commerce. When more broadly defined, however, culture includes religion. And holidays and traditions in many cultures are inextricably tied to religion.

Is it a good thing for Christian parents to expose their young children to other religions? I don't believe it is.

Our children can be taught that other religions exist and as they grow older they should be taught what other religions espouse. These are objective, rational, informational lessons, worthy of being taught to children who are capable of learning them in an objective, rational, information-focused way. But that isn't what happens when children are exposed to other religions *early in life* and on an emotional level.

Consider how your child is learning to worship as a Christian. He or she is likely learning songs, attending services and following whatever ritual is involved, learning to recognize and manipulate certain symbols associated with the church, hearing Bible stories and memorizing simple verses. Your child is learning first and foremost the "language" of Christianity and the repeated forms of Christian behavior. Both the language and behavior are laden with values that are reinforced.

When a young child repeatedly watches a program that is rooted in a different religion (even if that religion is atheism or the program claims to be completely secular), your child is being exposed to the language and rituals of that religion on an intuitive, emotional level.

Children who watch *Mighty Morphin Power Rangers* know the "liturgy" of the program. They know to stand and hold out their Power Morphin coins and say, "It's morphin time." They know next to call out the name of their power-source dinosaur or other creature. They know next to start doing karate moves, reach for their magic weapons, and call greater powers until they are fully empowered to defeat their enemies. When certain music begins to play, specifically, "Go, go, Power Rangers" or "We are VR," they know the time has come for fighting.

A ritualistic pattern was established, one not rooted in Christian values, but in Eastern philosophy, particularly the rituals of Japanese secularism and communal ritual. In other words, the "religion" of modern Japan.

Consider the real essence of Japanese religious life in today's world. While Shintoism may still technically be considered the main religion of Japan, few modern Japanese consider themselves actively involved in Shinto rituals. Worship of ancestors is largely left for formal state functions involving the Emperor and his family. The real religion of Japan today can be summed up in two phrases:

1. Be Part of the Group.

The Japanese philosophy is one of doing things *together* for the good of the whole. If you're "in," you're "in," and everyone else is "out" of your particular group, company, neighborhood, or the nation itself. Conformity is stressed. Among the Japanese, those born and raised in the United States are refered to differently than Japanese who are born and raised in Japan.

This aspect of Power Rangers is especially strong. "If you aren't a Power Ranger, you're a nobody." In fact, you're either stupid (as in the case of Bulk and Skull), or you are virtually invisible (just try to name one other student at Angel Grove High School besides Bulk and Skull).

The Power Rangers are often called to a "group meeting" with Zordon. They operate with an understanding of what to do. They always fight together, even though one or two may be forced to fight individually at the onset of a skirmish. They maintain close contact with one another and form a closed group. They may belong to other clubs, but ultimately, no one else can belong to the Power Rangers' group unless chosen and authorized by Zordon.

2. Use Power for Your Group's Advantage.

The Japanese are intent on winning and controlling. They do not share power or markets readily. Many Japanese openly advocate world domination by their culture.

Japanese cartoons are nearly always focused on saving the world—not a neighborhood, city, area, or particular people. The Japanese think globally, and when they do, they think of themselves as being in charge and the world running according to Japanese principles, methods, and protocol. When Japanese cartoon and live-action TV programs are adapted to an American children's audience, the programs may feature American-looking and American-sounding heroes, but the methods and ideology are still very Japanese: be part of a group, and make sure your group wins.

Secular vs. Religious Groups

In keeping with the secularism of Japan today, the groups to which the Japanese belong are highly secular: corporations, clubs, organizations, and so forth. This secularization is obvious in Japanese children's programming. The "dojo"—the center where karate is taught— and the nonaligned, a-religious "youth center" are two places children meet. Power Rangers and VR Troopers apparently never go home because we never see their families. What we do see is a family-like atmosphere at the karate gym and the youth center juice bar.

Is this the cultural climate we want to present to our young children as being ideal? Where's the church? Where are the people who worship God and abide by His commandments rather than the beck and call of a bodiless talking head named Zordon? Where do older and younger people fit into this world?

Mighty Morphin Catechism

Programs such as *Mighty Morphin Power Rangers* and *VR Troopers* are rooted in a "catechism" that promotes Eastern religions.

Much of any religion has to do with the issue of power—what it is, who has it, how one gets it, how it works. The perception of power in these two programs is rooted in the idea that a person is his own savior and supreme being. That is a common thread in all Eastern religions. Qualities of spiritual greatness are said to lie within and need only to be released. How the power is released results in the different doctrines and variations on the general Eastern theme.

Christianity advocates that spiritual power is resident in God, and that God's presence and power can be invited to indwell a person through believing in Jesus Christ, repenting of sins, and receiving the Holy Spirit. Christianity provides for a free-will acceptance of God's power into one's life. At no time, however, does the person "conjure" that power.

Eastern religions and occult practices recognize that power resides outside the individual. But that power is always regarded as a neutral force. Therefore, it is something "good" into which a person should tap.

Christianity says that there is "evil power" resident in Satan and his demon cohorts. Those who tap into evil power use it for evil means and become evil in the process. Those who tap into God's pure and holy power use it for good.

Spiritism at Work

Spiritism is the oldest form of religion on earth. Virtually every religion today, other than Judaism and Christianity, is rooted in spiritism. The seven basic principles of spiritism are:

1. There is a supreme father.
2. All men are created equal brothers.
3. Life is a continuous existence.
4. Man follows an endless progression.

5. A person's walk along that path is his or her responsibility.
6. Communion with spirits can help.
7. There are rewards for those who follow good.

One of the most common spiritism derivatives in the United States is the Americanized version of Hinduism. Hinduism seeks to include all religions into some type of oneness. It claims there is a god in everything and an amorphous universal god spirit that can pervade any substance. It stands in direct opposition to the Judeo-Christian concept of One True and Living God.

Hinduism challenges one to move toward perfection by following an Eight-Fold Path: right belief, right resolve, right word, right act, right life, right effort, right thinking, right meditation. To follow this path, one develops a unique spirit. Each individual is totally responsible for his salvation. There is no such thing as sin because there is no absolute standard for holiness.

Many symbols are used in spiritism, including circles and triangles in various combinations, all-seeing eyes, and rays of light. Spiritism includes these concepts that are prevalent in children's programming today:

the third eye	magic
astral projection	"the force"
mental telepathy	wizardry
tascended masters	clairvoyance

When one places *Mighty Morphin Power Rangers* and *VR Troopers* next to the template of spiritism, it's impossible to avoid the fact that these programs are rooted and steeped in Eastern religion. A number of very specific spiritism practices and symbols are employed by these programs, including the following:

Animal Power

One of the most common figures of ancient paganism is the half-human, half-animal figure. The famous god Dagon (of the Philistines) was half-beast, half-man/god.

Mighty Morphin Power Rangers asks children to "play" at becoming one in spirit with creatures. The first season, these creatures were long-dead dinosaur "powers." The power of these creatures was assumed to be active, even though the creatures are long since extinct. In the more recent series of programs, the spirits of existing animals, such as wolf and tiger, are evoked. The concept is rooted in the *belief* that power is universal and can be tapped, regardless of source.

The premise that a group of teenagers, "dinosaur spirits," and "amazing robots" can protect the earth is not only far-fetched, but an insidious thought to plant in the minds of children.

Masks

Masks play an important role in pagan religions and represent more than just a change in one's appearance. They are believed to be a direct link to the spirit world and a means to channel supernatural forces. Masks are directly related to a person's ability to "transform." When a person dons a mask, he or she takes on a new personality, abilities, and "spirit."

Morphing is nothing more than "donning a mask," with all of the inherent spiritual power intended!

Rainbow Colors

In Eastern religion, the rainbow is not a symbol of God's promise never again to destroy earth by water. Rather, the rainbow symbolizes that, "all colors are equal and should be united in harmony." The New Age adopted the rainbow as its symbol of equal brotherhood of all mankind. When characters in children's programming take on a rainbow of colors, be wary. The message being reinforced over and over is that those with various rainbow colors are good and helpful.

Power Ranger teens are colorful when they are "transformed" into their Ranger identities. They battle evil Putties—gray creatures without distinctive features. The Power Rangers' foremost weapon shoots colorful laser rays of destruction. (Light is a big part of the "power" manifestation in the *Mighty Morphin Power Rangers* episodes. In fact, the logo for Power Rangers is a modified, rather "fat" lightning bolt. Lightning routinely signals the appearance of thunderzord power.)

Although the VR Troopers are less colorful, they still have far more color than their black Skug enemies.

Scrying

Scrying is the practice of seeing, often into the future. It is a type of divination that usually employs transparent materials such as water, crystals, mirrors, or crystal balls. Power Rangers look through Zordon's magic glass to watch behind-the-scene activities of Rita Repulsa or Lord Zed. Rita Repulsa has her own "telescope" from the moon to earth.

Magic Wands

Paganism nearly always involves ritual that includes the manipulation of magical tools and symbols for supernatural purposes. Magic wands are the most common example. These items are frequently employed as part of an incantation and transformation process.

Power Rangers have Power Morphin coins. VR Troopers have virtual reality pendants. Each must be grasped and held high during an incantation to release power. They are futuristic versions of magic wands.

Karl Zictor, enemy of VR Troopers, has a crystal ball used for transformation.

Astral Projection

In this process, using a figure of light, human beings project themselves through space to a location away from their actual location. Power Rangers regularly project themselves to and from Command Center meetings with Zordon and Alpha 5.

Familiars

Common in virtually all pagan and occult practices, familiars are animals that supposedly have demonic spirit power to assist a person in supernatural activities. Karl Zictor's iguana plays the role of a familiar in *VR Troopers*. Zictor frequently strokes his iguana named "Juliet" before transforming into Grimlord.

Incantations

One of the oldest beliefs in cultures around the world is that the real name of something enshrines both its essence and its power. From this perspective, words become weapons or tools of power. Language is a prime tool of sorcery, mainly through incantations.

Power Rangers say, "It's morphin time," followed by, "Power Rangers." Then each Power Ranger recites the power source he or she wishes to tap: Tyrannosaur, Pterodactyl, Saber-toothed Tiger, and so forth. When they combine their powers to create Megazord, they do so by using the incantation, "Power up!"

When the wicked Karl Zictor transforms into Grimlord, he says an incantation as he touches his crystal ball: "Forces of darkness, empower me. Take me back to my virtual reality."

Nothing left to the imagination there!

Possession

The goal of most occult practices is taking on a more powerful identity. The reason underscoring the acquiescence to demonic power is the desire to have Satan's power at work in one's life. This possession is openly portrayed in many cartoons, usually by glowing red eyes and lightening bolts emanating from the possessed person. These are routine occurrences for the evil lords and the monsters they create on *Mighty Morphin Power Rangers* and *VR Troopers*.

What is particularly insidious is that Power Rangers or VR Troopers don't need to be "open" to evil in any way before they are caught in its clutches.

Power Rangers can be arbitrarily zapped by Rita Repulsa or Lord Zed to do their bidding. Tommy is reeled into Rita's control in the Green Ranger series called "Green with Evil." Billy is locked into Rita's spell of fear against his will. Both Billy and Zack are forced to wear goggles that make everyone appear to be Putties. There's a real flaw in logic here. One might ask, "What keeps Rita from exerting absolute power by casting a spell over all five Power Rangers at one time?"

The same is true for VR Troopers. J. B. is sucked into the computer against his will while he tries to help a friend with a computer problem.

In this, the purveyors of the occult skewed the message for a double deception: evil can possess us against our will. Such a concept only evokes fear, not true understanding.

On the other hand, possession is very real and it isn't limited only to make-believe monsters.

When Magic Poses as Reality . . .

Leading occultists do not differentiate white magic from black magic. They perceive only magic. The Bible also makes no distinction between white and black magic.

Programs such as *Mighty Morphin Power Rangers* and *VR Troopers* have significantly blurred the lines. The good guys and bad guys all use the same methods. One group only has a little more "power" than the other.

Gone, too, is any notion of these stories being told in "once upon a time" terms, a surefire cue to a child that he is embarking on a fantasy.

Are Rangers real? To a young child they are.

Is there really a Command Center, a robot named Alpha 5, and Zordon the omniscient? To a young child, there is.

A young child has no way of knowing that these people and places don't exist. That's a concept we adults forget all too often.

It is equally impossible for a child to differentiate between what is sacred and what is not. Your child does not know he is watching occult practices. He doesn't know that he's being entertained by programs grounded in spiritism and new brands of Hinduism. From his perspective, he's watching a slice of life.

Turn Off the Evil Spell

If your answer to any of these questions is "yes," turn off the program your child is watching:

1. **Are there demons, spirits, or familiars that help certain characters achieve their goals?**

2. **Does the program have wizards, witches, or spirits as good guys?**

3. **Does the program employ occult symbols?**

4. **Does the program depict occult practices, such as seeing through crystal balls, levitation, mind control, divination, or astral projection?**

5. **Do the characters use the tools of witchcraft or the occult, such as wearing amulets or using magic wands, incantations, or spells?**

Our children are being taught by TV today to call on demons for power.

What if one answers?

11

Fueling the Lust for Power

Every child seeks mastery over his world. He desires to hold his own against persons older or bigger than himself. She desires abilities that are just beyond her grasp.

In many ways, the desire for power is part of us from birth. It may very well be one of the "drives" that compels us toward growth and development.

What differentiates a normal desire for power, however, from a *lust* for power are these two main qualities:
  • the person who *lusts* for power wants *absolute* power—power that results in total control and total elimination of all enemies.
  • the person who *lusts* for power wants *universal* power—power that works in all situations against all obstacles.

Sometimes a person will enlist the help of others (be they fellow teens, allies, zords, or monsters) to help achieve this power.

The lust for power can never be satiated. Karl Zictor, the evil focus on *VR Troopers* says it well when he asks, "What does a person who has power over half the world desire?" The answer? "Power over the other half."

The lust for power nearly always manifests itself as the ability to manipulate and control other people.

Normal power

Normal power might be classified as that which is situational. A person desires enough power to get out of a jam, resolve a need, solve a problem, or get through a difficulty. These situations come and go.

Once the troublesome situation is past, a person is usually willing to relinquish power in order to "get along" with others and live in harmony. The normal flow of power among people is balanced by a spirit of compromise and mutual acceptance.

Lust for power

A lust for power is a desire to have maximum power in all situations. It goes far beyond need-meeting or problem-solving. There is no compromise with anyone, on any point, for any length of time.

A lust for power grows in intensity.

Mighty Morphin Power Rangers and VR Troopers are characters that exhibit lust for power. When they are strong, their enemies become stronger, requiring that they become even stronger.

What signals does this type of program send to a child?

It sends the signal to a child that his power will increase as the result of what he does.

Christianity teaches that power is "bestowed" by God, at God's discretion, although the person must willingly invite God's presence into his or her life. A person does not have the authority or ability to *demand* increased power. In fact, demanding power over another person is expressly forbidden, as is manipulation of others. Even in the cases where the apostles of Jesus cast out demons, they exhibited power over *spirits*, maintaining love and concern for the person possessed. As soon as the person was freed from possession, the apostles relinquished any power over the person.

A child does not have the prerogative to demand power over other children or adults.

Programs such as these send the signal to a child that he has a capacity for unlimited power.

In essence, the child can become omnipotent.

God alone is omnipotent. God alone has the wisdom necessary for the execution of absolute power.

Programs such as these feed a child's egocentricity and their innate belief that the world should revolve around their desires.

These programs convey the message to a child that good guys can never be defeated.

That simply isn't true—and it's a cruel fantasy to portray to a child. The assumption too readily drawn is that people who are accidently killed, or suffer disease, or have accidents must be bad guys, because good guys don't lose or experience trouble. Mighty Morphin Power Rangers and VR Troopers are not only examples of good winning over evil, but of good winning over evil without consequence. It's amazing to watch, but Power Rangers and Troopers take hits identical to those inflicted on their enemies, but Power Rangers and VR Troopers never get cuts, scrapes, bruises, or other injuries. They remain unscathed, while their enemies are pulverized into thin air.

The triumph of good over evil is a timeless story line. There's nothing wrong with good winning over evil. But good rarely wins without taking a hit. The reality of life is that good people suffer bad circumstances, endure bad situations, and sometimes fall victim to bad people. From the perspective of Power Rangers and VR Troopers, Christian martyrs may very well appear to have been bad-guy Putties.

Power Fuel

Several techniques are used to add "energy" to a film or video. One of them is the rapid cutting of visuals. The more rapid the cutting from scene to scene, the more excitement evoked.

Another technique is the use of sound or light "bursts"—explosions, lightning bolts, loud noises, claps of thunder. Even rapidly twinkling lights can give a sense of energy.

Perhaps the most potent energy fuel, however, is music underscore. The driving beat of Power Rangers is hard rock music. The synthesized music has no lyrics other than the frequently chanted, "Go, go, Power Rangers." It provides a steady, high-energy, throbbing undercurrent.

Power Rangers are not the first to use rock music. For years, Saturday-morning cartoons featuring rock bands would often emerge. These bands were mostly parody groups based on the Beatles, Monkeys, Jackson 5, or similar groups. Other cartoons had fictitious bands, such as Josie and the Pussycats. Rock music even showed up in *The Muppet Show*. Since the mid 1980s, however, music made for preteens and young children has taken a drastic turn. Electronic rhythms, heavy drumbeat, and the special effects of contemporary rock music are all included. The result is more than underscore to enhance visual images. This music drives the plot forward with its incessant, pounding beat.

Teenage Mutant Ninja Turtles were perhaps the first to use rock music extensively. Power Rangers picked up where they left off. And now, VR Troopers videos include an MTV-style "video" at the end of each story line—a rock song with little more than a lengthy series of explosions and combat sequences as visuals.

What is the purpose of rock music in *Power Rangers* and *VR Troopers?* The music plays two main roles. First, it commands attention and focuses concentration. This music almost lulls young children to stare at the screen. It is repetitive and loud. Nothing else in a room is likely to distract a child who is listening to it. It forces the child to attend to the visuals.

Second, the music energizes the visuals. In fact, turn off the volume and most of the visuals look inane, even to many children. The fight scenes look more disjointed, the monsters look more clumsy and stupid, and the attack sequences look more fake. But with the volume on, the scenes have momentum. The driving beat energizes the viewer and give a false sense of "power"—the very message of the show.

Children watching Power Rangers rarely sit still. They fidget, move, and want to engage in the action. Before long, and often even before the program ends, they are imitating the actions of their heroes on the screen. A child who is all jazzed up after such a program is not likely to turn off the set and read a book or play quietly with a toy. There is too much energy kindled for that! Rather, the child is likely to engage in activity to spend some of that energy—and often that behavior involves conflict, destruction, aggression, or intense physical expressions.

Rock music feeds the lust for power.

Turn Down the Volume

When it comes to Power Rangers and VR Troopers, my hearty suggestion is that you simply turn off these programs and turn off their influence. But the message of this chapter goes deeper than that.

Turn off all the "volume" in your young child's life. Monitor what your children hear, as much as what they watch.

From time-to-time, turn off the radio as often or more often than you turn off the television.

Maintain control over your child's selection of CDs or audio cassettes. This is your privilege and your responsibility as a parent. For as long as you have responsibility for your child—legally, financially, materially—you have authority over your child. What is played in your home, even through headsets, is part of your home's atmosphere. Don't allow your child to listen to music with ungodly lyrics that promote rebellion or selfish behavior. And I recommend that you guard your child, including your teenage children, against heavy rock music. The driving beat of this music is intended for only one purpose: to raise your child's excitement level. If a child doesn't have a healthy outlet for this energy, such as a sporting activity, it is likely to erupt in aggression or overt sexual behavior.

Children grow and develop healthier in calm and stable environments. Children naturally create enough noise of their own. They don't need to be steeped in a noisy environment.

Talk About Power Moves

Talk to your child about power—its uses, aberrations, benefits, potential for harm, underlying motivations, and abuses. Talk about how power can be harnessed, focused, and increased.

Power itself is a neutral force. It is energy, ability, and strength. It can be used for good or evil in a wide variety of ways—not just the limited ways portrayed in programs such as *Mighty Morphin Power Rangers* and *VR Troopers*. Help your child become power savvy without relying on fantasy examples of power.

Discuss the kind of power that is evident in the world and the kind of power your children will need to use, now, and as they grow to be adults. Don't allow virtual power or unrealistic superhero behavior to be your child's only examples of power at work.

Real power is God at work. Focus on Him.

Kimberly

Jason

12

7 More Reasons Not to Watch

In the last five chapters, I gave you the top five reasons parents should turn off *Mighty Morphin Power Rangers* and *VR Troopers* and refrain from purchasing products associated with them.

There are seven additional reasons these programs are unworthy of viewing time. In many ways, these reasons are no less potent than those in prior chapters. But they can be stated more directly, simply, and succinctly. Any *one* of these is good enough reason for protecting a child against the influence of these violent, Eastern superheroes.

1. Low Production Values.

These programs simply aren't very good television.

The programs have sparse dialogue and little acting apart from the martial arts choreography. The effects include lots of fire, smoke (CO_2), and general destruction of property to cover poor design.

The sets are cheap. Many scenes look like they were shot at a Burbank landfill. The monsters are even cheaper. They make the original Godzilla and King Kong look good. Rita Repulsa's words are rarely in "sync" with her lip movements.

The producers make no apologies for the low production value of the program. They call this programs' signature "primitive feel."[1]

Sad to say, the show's success spawned some knock-off shows, such as *Superhuman Samurai Syber Squad* and *Tattooed Teen-age Alien Fighters from Beverly Hills* (USA). Although it may not seem possible to an adult viewer, these spin-off shows have characters that wear even cheaper costumes, special effects that are less convincing, the acting is more wooden, and the monsters are cheaper in appearance and clumsier in motion.

It is demeaning and offensive to our children when producers give anything other than their finest effort to children's programs. Our children should be presented the finest television has to offer—the funniest programs, the most inspiring dramas, the most sparkling music, the most brilliant acting, directing, lighting, choreography, and costuming.

Why play to the lowest common denominator? Why give "schlocky" TV to kids? (The TV executive's answer, of course, is that children can't tell the difference, so why spend more in getting them to clamor for specific products, toys, and cereals?)

Our children need to be elevated in importance and played "up to," not "down to."

2. Only Perfect People.

I object that the good guys in these programs are depicted as flawless. Teens in *Mighty Morphin Power Rangers* and *VR Troopers* are handsome and pretty—there's only one pair of eyeglasses in the lot and that pair is worn by the "science whiz" of the Rangers. The teens are popular, smart, and well-dressed. The human bad guys—apart from the monsters, ghouls, and gremlins of the mythical evil empires—are nerds and bullies, who are slovenly, poorly-dressed, fat, ugly, and unpopular.

This sends an unhealthy esteem message to children who are less than perfect, shy, or do not have many friends.

I want my children to admire people for what they do in *real life situations*, not for what they look like, dream about, or do in the privacy of their own dream worlds.

3. Sexual Overtones.

I react very strongly to the use of sex to sell product to children. Power Ranger and VR Trooper teens are highly sexual and act in sexual ways toward one another, especially the flirtation between Kimberly, Pink Ranger, and Tommy, Green/White Ranger. The teens regularly wear shorts and tank tops, all the better to show off their perfect muscles and cute figures.

Many parents refuse to face the fact that young children are sexual beings. Children are subject to sexual titillation and stimulation, and they can be easily aroused sexually by material that has heavy sexual content.

Many of the Mighty Morphin Power Ranger and VR Trooper behaviors are teenage behaviors—ones that are not appropriate for children. Thus, they have no place in children's programs.

4. Disregard for Authority.

As previously mentioned, Putties are as likely to be policemen as they are businessmen before they transform into Putties. The principal of Angel Grove High School, where the Power Rangers attend, is clumsy and nearly always made to appear out-of-touch, out-of-"synch," and out-of-date. He is the brunt of jokes. *Mighty Morphin Power Rangers* holds a general disregard for natural, human authority.

5. A Heavy Emphasis on Stereotypes.

As politically correct as these programs attempt to be, they still portray numerous stereotypes. Scientists are nerds, unless they are into cool things like computers and supernatural gadgetry. Teachers are women, but principals are men. Bullies are fat or dumb.

Trini and Kimberly, and later Kimberly and Aisha play the role of "encouragers" in many scenes to the stronger, more dominant, and more decisive male Power Rangers.

In the original Power Rangers cast, Caucasian Kimberly is given the color Pink. Oriental Trini, Yellow. And African-American Zack, Black. Talk about stereotyping!

6. A Negative Bias Against Business.

Some story lines for *Mighty Morphin Power Rangers* and *VR Troopers* involves pollution of the environment by Rita Repulsa, as well as by human culprits. In *VR Troopers*, the bad guy is a mega-millionaire corporate executive.

In most instances, big business is presented as *the* foremost evil force behind pollution and wasting of energy and environmental resources.

The only business people of merit in the programs I have seen are Ernie, who runs a small juice bar in the youth center frequented by Power Rangers, and the dojo instructors, especially Tao of *VR Troopers*. And they are never shown ringing up a sale!

7. A strong one-world sentiment.

It's not enough that Power Rangers and VR Troopers defend the entire world. VR Troopers live in peaceful Crossworld City.

The one-world sentiment undergirding these programs is profound. Zordon is a type of one-world ruler. Rita Repulsa, Lord Zed, and Grimlord all aspire to be one-world rulers.

Children of all cultures are portrayed in these programs as being united, of one purpose, and responding to one set of values and one ethical code. It is only one small step to the assumption that such children would have the same religion and give loyalty to the same leader.

On the Whole . . .

If these seven reasons, plus the previous five reasons, are *not* sufficient reasons for you to turn off these programs in your home, ask yourself: "Can I name twelve *good* reasons for my child to watch these programs day in and day out?"

Ask yourself, "Would I want my child to *be* a Power Ranger or a VR Trooper?"

I suspect your answer would be "no."

At least I hope it would be.

Part 3

What's A Parent To Do?

13

Ten Things You Can Do to Save Your Child from these "Saviors" of the Planet

Let me leave you with a word of encouragement: your children can grow up to be happy, healthy, spiritually-alive, productive citizens without ever watching even one minute of *Mighty Morphin Power Rangers* or *VR Troopers* programs.

A Christian man once asked me, "Doesn't my child need to be aware that these toys and shows are out there in order to fully be part of his generation and culture?"

In a word, "No."

There's nothing about these programs that is necessary to your child's development, faith, or ability to relate to other people in a kind, generous, cooperative way.

I encouraged this man to ask different questions of himself. "Do you really want your child to mimic the culture at large? Do you want your child to be an average member of his or her generation?"

As a Christian parent, I trust your answer will be, "No, I want my child to follow Christ and be "salt" and "light" in this world. I want my child to be a leader when it comes to setting the ethical and moral standards of his generation."

In a very positive, pro-Christ way, there are at least 10 things you can do to help your child when it comes to media and toy selection.

1. Limit your child's TV time.

Know when a television set is on in your house, and know what is being viewed. As a good parent, you monitor the food that goes into your child's mouth. You are concerned about the quality of your child's education. Take responsibility and be equally concerned about the behaviors, ethics, and spiritual values that are being fed to your child's mind and spirit in the guise of entertainment.

Have a strict rule that of no TV viewing before school, during meals, or before homework is complete. That rule alone would eliminate most occult-based and violent programs aired during "children's time slots."

2. Avoid programs with violence, horror, sexual content, or occult symbols and activity.

If you have doubt about a program, watch at least three episodes of it prior to allowing your child to watch the show.

One of the best ways to regulate what your child watches in advance of viewing is to get a monitor-only system for the "TV" set your child is allowed to watch. A monitor plays videotapes but does not receive broadcast or cable programs. Rent or purchase videos you believe are suitable and show them to your child at a time convenient to your family's schedule.

I recommend that preschoolers not be allowed to watch more than thirty minutes of TV a day.

3. Make a no-TV rule for a designated night or nights of the week.

Call these exploring days or activity days. Do something fun and active with your child, even if its only to walk around your neighborhood or a family bicycle ride.

4. When you do watch TV, make the viewing a family activity.

Watch programs with your child. That way, you are there to turn off the set if something offensive is aired, or to answer questions and inspire your child to think beyond the immediate plot to consequences and possible alternative choices of behavior. I do *not* recommend that children or teens have their own television sets to watch in the privacy of their bedrooms.

5. Encourage watching a wide variety of programs.

Watch nature programs together, sports programs, how-to programs (a good alternative to Saturday morning cartoons), and old classic TV shows and movies from decades past.

6. Place higher value on activities that truly promote learning, creativity, and socialization.

Consider requiring that your child spend at least one hour reading or in free-form play, alone or with friends, for every half-hour of TV viewing allowed.

7. Talk about what you see.

If your child questions your decision about a program, be able to explain why you do or do not like it. When a program coincides with your family's viewpoints or value structure, tell your child why. Be sure to talk about the commercials, too.

8. Model activities other than TV watching.

Many children assume that TV is the "preferred method of entertainment" because they see their parents watching television as *their* primary form of relaxing. Model other activities before your child. Whenever possible, invite your child to participate in alternate forms of recreation—perhaps a sport or exercise such as swimming or cycling; board or certain card games, or reading stories aloud to one another. Be creative and seek variety in how you spend your time.

9. Provide good media materials for your child other than videos.

Choose child-oriented computer programs carefully, including CD Roms. Help your child choose Christ-honoring music. Subscribe to magazines that present wholesome values. Take your child to the library often and help him or her build a personal library of favorite books to read.

10. Buy toys with high "play" value.

These are toys that are notable for their:

- ability to evoke a child's creativity and imagination (such as dolls with no names, crayons, art and craft kits)
- ability to promote reasoning or learning skills (such as play-school materials, puzzles, and games rooted in logic, memory, and perception skills)
- durability over time
- use in *active* play (toys that cause your child to move, such as tricycles, pull toys, baby gyms; and for older children, various types of sporting gear, wagons, bicycles)
- mirror of the real world (such as kitchen, tool, and science sets)
- value-free nature (toys that allow your child to use in make-believe plots of their own creation, such as dress-up items, plush toys, drama play kits)
- safety (a toy that doesn't require constant supervision by an adult and is age-appropriate)

Remember that children are *Not* the best choosers of their toys. You are! And, children do not need a lot of toys. Cycle toys so only a few are available for play on any given day or during any given week.

You Are Your Child's Best "Entertainment"

You are far more interesting to your child than you may think you are. If given a choice, most children would rather spend time with a loving, encouraging, supportive parent than with a television set or toy. Make yourself available to your child—to answer questions, converse, and play. Get down on the floor and play *with* your child and his or her toys. Go outside and play catch or give your child a push on the swing set.

Take your child with you to church—also, when you do volunteer work (if appropriate), and when you go shopping.

Involve your child, according to his or her developmental skills when you do chores—including cooking, cleaning, yard work, and simple home repairs.

Teach your child "as you go."

In so doing, you'll give your child information and teach him or her how to use that information and discard that which is unnecessary or harmful. You'll be teaching your child the values you hold most important in a natural, unpreachy manner.

Above all, preserve your child's innocence and purity. Don't let your child become a dumpster for the world's garbage.

You have the potential to be a far more powerful force in your child's life than any Power Ranger. You *are* more real to your child than any VR Trooper can ever be. In other words, to your child, you have all it takes to be a superhero—by being a good parent!

References

Chapter 4

1 Roberts, Irving , *What's Selling,* Playthings, December 1994, p. 15.

2 Gamlin, Joanne , *What's Selling,* Playthings, December 1994, p. 17.

3 Wanderer, Robert , *What's Selling,* Playthings, December 1994,p. 18

4 Johns, Reid, *What's Selling,* Playthings, December 1994, p. 18.

5 Warrick, Pamela , *Power Outage,* Los Angeles Times, December 23, 1993.

Chapter 6

1 Graham, Jefferson, *Syndicators Scan Japan for Cartoons,* USA Today, January 20, 1995, p. 3D.

2 Ibid.

Chapter 7

1 Hull, Bryson and Hatlestad, Lucas , *No, No, Power Rangers?* Parenting, February 1995, p. 82.

2 Ibid.

3 Ibid.

4 Edwards, Ellen , The Fox in the Children's Coop— *Margaret Loesch and the Mighty Morphin Kids Network,* The Washington Post, May 26, 1994, p. d1.

5 Leccese, Donna, *Toymakers Wary of '95,* Playthings, January 1995, pp. 34-35.

6 Siegel, Alberta, *The Effects of Media Violence on Social Learning,* p. 85.

7 As reported in USA Today, October 21, 1993, p. 1.

8 U.S. News and World Report, December 26, 1994, p. 111.

9 Phillips, Phil, *Saturday Morning Mind Control,* Thomas Nelson Publishers, 1991, p. 64.

Chapter 10

1 Licensing Scope, *Saban's Power Rangers continue to dominate,* Playthings, February 1994, p. 125.

2 Graham, Jefferson, *Syndicators Scan Japan for Cartoons,* USA Today, January 20, 1995, p. 3D.

Chapter 12

1 McCormick, Patricia S., *The Power That Be,* Fort Worth Star Telegram, February 13, 1995.

Other Books by Starburst Publishers

(Partial listing—full list available on request)

The Truth About Power Rangers —Phil Phillips

An in-depth look at the Mighty Morphin Power Rangers, revealing the violence and philosophy behind the #1 toy and kids' TV show in America. Power Rangers are leaping off toystore shelves and kicking their way into the minds of millions of children. This book explores the Power Rangers phenomena and the impact they have on children.

(trade paper) ISBN 0914984675 **$6.95**

Dinosaurs, The Bible, Barney & Beyond —Phil Phillips

In-depth look at Evolution, Creation Science, and Dinosaurs in the media and toys. Reader learns why Barney, the oversized purple dinosaur, has become a pal to millions of children, and what kind of role model is Barney.

(trade paper) ISBN 0914984594 **$9.95**

Horror And Violence —The Deadly Duo In The Media —Phil Phillips and Joan Hake Robie

Americans are hooked on violence! Muggings, kidnappings, rape and murders are commonplace via your TV set. This book not only brings you up-to-date on what is happenig in the media in general, but also will help you and your children survive with integrity in a complex media environment.

(trade paper) ISBN 0914984160 **$9.95**

Turmoil In The Toy Box —Phil Phillips

A shocking exposé of the toy and cartoon industry—unmasks the New Age, Occult, Violent, and Satanic influences that have invaded the once innocent toy box. Over 175,000 in print.

(trade paper) ISBN 0914984047 **$9.95**

Halloween And Satanism —Phil Phillips and Joan Hake Robie

This book traces the origins of Halloween and gives the true meaning behind this celebration of "fun and games." Jack-O-Lanterns, Cats, Bats, and Ghosts are much more than costumes and window decorations. In this book you will discover that involvement in any form of the occult will bring you more than "good fortune." It will lead you deeper and deeper into the Satanic realm, which ultimately leads to death. Over 90,000 in print.

(trade paper) ISBN 091498411X **$9.95**

Teenage Mutant Ninja Turtles Exposed! —Joan Hake Robie

Looks closely at the national popularity of Teenage Mutant Ninja Turtles. Tells what they teach and how this "turtle" philosophy affects children (and adults) mentally, emotionally, socially, morally, and spiritually. The book gives the answer to what we can do about the problem.

(trade paper) ISBN 0914984314 **$5.95**

Books by Starburst Publishers—cont'd.

Angels, Angels, Angels
—Phil Phillips

Subtitled—*Embraced by The Light...or...Embraced by The Darkness?* Discovering the truth about Angels, Near-Death Experiences and other Spiritual Awakenings. Also, why the sudden interest in angels in this day and age? Can we trust what we read in books like *Embraced By The* Light?

(trade paper) ISBN 0914984659 **$10.95**

Beyond The River
—Gilbert Morris & Bobby Funderburk

The first novel of *The Far Fields* series, **Beyond the River** makes for intriguing reading with high spiritual warfare impact. Set in the future and in the mode of *Brave New World* and *1984*, **Beyond The River** presents a world that is ruined by modern social and spiritual trends. This anti-utopian novel offers an excellent opportunity to speak to the issues of the New Age and "politically-correct" doctrines that are sweeping the country.

(trade paper) ISBN 0914984519 **$8.95**

TemperaMysticism
—Shirley Ann Miller

Subtitled—Exploding The Temperament Theory. Former Astrologer reveals how Christians (including some well-respected leaders) are being lured into the occult by practicing the Temperaments (Sanguine, Choleric, Phlegmatic, and Melancholy) and other New Age personality typologies.

(trade paper) ISBN 0914984306 **$8.95**

Political Correctness Exposed
—Marvin Sprouse

Subtitled—*A Piranha in Your Bathtub.* Explores the history of Political Correctness, how it originated, who keeps it alive today, and more importantly, how to combat Political Correctness. Contains 25 of the most frequently-told Politically Correct lies.

(trade paper) ISBN 0914984624 **$9.95**

Purchasing Information

Listed books are available from your favorite Bookstore, either from current stock or special order. To assist bookstore in locating your selection be sure to give title, author, and ISBN #. If unable to purchase from the bookstore you may order direct from STARBURST PUBLISHERS. When ordering enclose full payment plus $2.50* for shipping and handling ($3.00* if Canada or Overseas). Payment in US Funds only. Please allow two to three weeks minimum (longer overseas) for delivery. Make checks payable to and mail to STARBURST PUBLISHERS, P.O. Box 4123, LANCASTER, PA 17604. Credit card orders may also be placed by calling 1-800-441-1456 (credit card orders only), Mon-Fri, 8 AM-5 PM Eastern Time. **Prices subject to change without notice.**   6-95